Lies From The Pulpit

Connie Wiedeman

PublishAmerica
Baltimore

First printing

ISBN: 1-4137-0454-9
PUBLISHED BY PUBLISHAMERICA, LLLP
www.publishamerica.com
Baltimore

Printed in the United States of America

INTRODUCTION

"I am firmly convinced that religions do harm as I am that they are untrue."
Nobel Prize Winning Author
Lord Bertrand Russell

Is your Pastor or Priest destroying your chance at salvation? If motives are right, do mere terms of doctrine matter? Most would answer in the negative to both of these questions; but that is not what the Bible teaches. How can we worship God, or accept Jesus as our Savior, if we lack a basic understanding of who They are? There can be no compromise...no "agreeing to differ"...upon the all-important theme of doctrine.

It is the Christian's duty and privilege to search the Bible, where God has revealed Himself and His purpose, so that they may know the God whom they worship. Failure to do so will render worship vain and useless and destroy any hope of personal salvation.

Christ's own words teach us that those who worship God must worship Him *in Truth.* (John 4:24). Those will perish who do not receive the word of the Truth...all that do not believe the Truth will be damned. (2 Thessalonians 2:10,12)

Most churches preach that God is made up of God the Father, God the Son, and God the Holy Spirit (or Ghost). Very few teach that the doctrine of the Trinity is false...that Jesus is the Son of God, not God the Son. *The ones who are in error cannot expect to attain eternal life,* no matter how sincere the belief. Unfortunately, as humans, we often reject anything that challenges our long-held, deeply rooted beliefs no matter how incorrect those beliefs or how correct the challenge. For those who are willing to seek the Truth, let us examine the falsehoods being taught about God and His Son, Jesus Christ; Immortality of the Soul; Heaven Going; Baptism; Death; God's Heavenly Kingdom; Hell; The Devil; Homosexuality; and other biblical matters.

Contents

THE LIE:
Once Saved, Always Saved
(Saying You Accept Jesus Christ Guarantees Salvation That Can Never Be Lost)

> "God so loved the world that He gave His only begotten Son, that whosoever believeth in Him shall not perish, but shall have everlasting life." (John 3:16)

This is probably Christendom's most quoted verse of Scripture. Yet, how many understand *all* that it says?

"If there is anyone here who has not accepted Jesus as their Savior, and wants to have eternal life, repeat after me:
'Thank you Jesus for forgiving my sins; I believe
you were born of the virgin Mary, died for my
sins, and rose again from the dead.'
If you have prayed that prayer, you will have eternal salvation and no one can snatch you from the hand of God."

That is what is described as an "altar call" and it, or something similar, is issued in most churches Sunday after Sunday. The clergy have their congregations believing that salvation is unconditional once this vow is taken. But that is not what the Bible tells us. John 3:16 gives us the *primary* condition upon which we can seek salvation...and there are others.

"God so loved the world..." God created this world and declared it "very good." It was without evil and without disaster. It was man that turned it into the sinful place that it is, and yet, we are told numerous times in His book, that God loved it and all that are in it.

It is God's *love* that is unconditional, not salvation.

"...that He gave His only begotten Son..." All Christians know that John 3:16 tells us that God sent His Son that we might have a way out of our sin, that we might have a way to eternal life. But it tells us *much more than that.*

We are told that, in spite of our natural fate...to perish...caused by Adam's sin, God has provided a way of salvation in spite of our sinfulness, and that way is through His begotten Son. Most of Christendom, however, teaches that Jesus is *God the Son,* not the *Son of God* that both Jesus and God tell us He is.

"...that whosoever believes in Him (Jesus)..." But how can we say that we believe in Him if we don't even know who He is?

"shall not perish..." Without this gift from God of His Son, we would have been condemned to perish; we would have had to look forward only to becoming completely destroyed, to decay beyond any usefulness.

In the Old Testament, we were told that God gave His people a chance to be saved. He provided that chance through Moses, with the Laws they should follow. Had they followed the law, they were assured that they could be saved.

But man, because of that sinful nature inherited from God's created son, Adam, could not follow the law, and God, because of his *love*, provided *another* way to salvation. He sent another Son, His only *begotten Son*, as a sacrifice for those who would believe in this Son.

Most of Christendom misses this message in several respects.

One, it believes *and teaches* that there is some part of man that survives death. That there is an immortal soul in man that flies off at the moment of death. (Discussed in a following chapter.)

Addendum A is a study of seven different translations of the Bible showing the various uses of the word "soul." I invite you to study this accumulation of Scriptures so that you will understand that the Bible defines itself, and in the Addendum, it certainly defines "soul."

As a result of the disobedience of God's first son, His *created* son, Adam, all generations after Adam were condemned to perish. The grave was to be their final destination. John 3:16 tells us that to perish is the natural fate of man *who does not accept Christ.*

"...but have everlasting life..." This one passage of the Bible tells us everything we need to know to be delivered from eternal death...from perishing. Yet the greatest questions of all are whether or not we understand the meaning of "believing in Him," and whether we even know who He is.

There is a great division in opinions among various denominations of Christendom as to what constitutes the belief sufficient to gain salvation.

Secondly, Christendom fails to understand what is meant by God's *begotten* Son. In spite of the clear biblical description of the virgin Mary being impregnated with the seed of God through His Holy Spirit...through His power...they teach that Jesus *is God*, come to earth through this virgin, and thus is God the Son. (More fully discussed in a following chapter).

Pastors, preachers, evangelists, or other church leaders, issue these altar calls to come forth and declare a belief in Jesus; then, when their invitations are accepted, tell the new Christian that he or she is assured that their salvation is secure; that they have done all that is necessary to enter into the Kingdom of God; that nothing can change their "saved" status; and that nothing more is required of them. The Scriptures prove this declaration of assured salvation to be false.

Salvation is very much conditional.

God makes it clear that, in order to be saved, we must be *born again;* that our lives must be changed by the belief we verbalize, or the belief is insufficient. (John 3:3)

> "In Christ Jesus, it is a new creature that counts." (Galatians 6:15)

If our belief...if our faith...is not sufficient to change our lives, then it is not sufficient to secure for us a place in the Kingdom. The belief necessary to obtain salvation, requires an on-going obedience to Jesus and His commandments. (1 John 2:4)

Because, under the Law, God had required that the Hebrews should use only a *perfect lamb* in their sacrifices, God, too, insisted on *perfection* in *His* sacrifice. Jesus is the only human that has ever lived a sinless life. Even though He was mortal; even though He was tempted; even though He *could have sinned*; He did not sin! He became God's perfect lamb, the Lamb of God, sacrificed for our sins, that whosoever believed in His Son, should not be among those who would otherwise perish, but instead would have everlasting life.

John 3:16 points out another thing. It tells us that God did not send Jesus to punish those who would *not* believe in Him. The punishment for non-belief had already been declared because of Adam's sin. That punishment was eternal death. What it says is that Jesus came so that those who *DID* believe in Him would receive a reward...life everlasting.

This raises a third issue. The failing of most of Christendom in not realizing the meaning of "believe."

We know that we cannot gain salvation by works, no matter how great the works; that works alone cannot assure us a place in the Kingdom. However, James 2:26 tells us such faith *without* works is dead.

Jesus, Himself, said that he who believes in Him will do the *works* that He does. (John 14:12). *He that says he knows Jesus but doesn't keep his commandments is a liar,* we're told in 1 John 2:4.

If our faith is sufficient to change our lives, then our faith will be manifested by our works, and will constitute the kind of faith God expects of His children, and they will dwell in His Kingdom forever. Death, the natural consequence of sin, will lose it's sting.

Jesus became the author of eternal salvation to all who *obey* Him, not to all who just *say* they believe in Him. No matter how many good works you do, just those good works will never gain you salvation. But works are important, because they are a reflection of what your faith really is. *Your faith is made perfect by your works.* (James 2:22)

There are many places in the Bible that say "Believe in Me and you are saved." I don't think there is disagreement with any of the members of Christendom that say that anyone who believes in Jesus may have eternal life. Our differences lie in the meaning and *quality* of the "belief" required.

There are no contradictions in the Bible, so we have to, then, understand that the word "belief" or "believe" has a special meaning that we do not normally attribute to it today. The quality of belief that we need for salvation is the belief that changes our lives.

When we are baptized into Christ, we are "*born again*" and our lives must show that we are then "*new creatures,*" living our lives through Christ. If we do not experience such a change in the things we do and say and think, then we have not had the quality of belief, required by God, that will result in our eternal salvation.

A search of the Scriptures assures us that it doesn't mean just reciting the words. James 2:22 tells us that by the believer's *works* his faith is *perfected.*

Jesus, Himself, told us that *if* we believe in Him, *we will do the works that He does*. In other words, if we *don't do the works* that He does, we don't believe in Him. It takes a special, life-changing kind of belief to gain salvation. Jesus said that unless a man be born again, he cannot see the Kingdom of God. (John 3:3)

> "Be careful to do good works, continually." (Titus 3:8)

Too many argue that "it" is a gift of God and that you don't have to earn a gift. Whether the "it" they refer to is the gift of salvation or whether it is the gift of His Son, a gift can be accepted, refused, rejected, returned, or it can be reclaimed by the giver if the conditions upon which it was made are not kept. Nor can it be forced upon someone who does not want it.

> "...love the Lord your God...then you shall live...but *if you turn away*...you shall surely perish." (Deuteronomy 30:16,17,18) "*Those who have forsaken the Lord* shall perish." *(Isaiah 1:28)*

The argument that salvation is "unconditional" has failed to recognize that John 3:16, itself, sets forth a condition...it is conditional upon belief in Jesus.

These were the words of Jesus, Himself, speaking to the believers of His day:

> "You (believers) are indeed the salt of the earth; but *if the salt should lose its savor*, with what could it be salted? It would not be worth anything but to be thrown outside and to be trodden down by men." (Matthew 5:13)

Man becomes the salt of the earth, in God's eyes, when he accepts Jesus as his Savior, but losing the fervor and the passion of his conversion, he becomes without savor and of no use to Jesus, either in this life or in the Kingdom; he will be good for nothing but to be thrown out, because his belief was not sufficient to *sustain* his faith.

> "Unless a man *remains with Me*," said Jesus, "he will be cast outside..." (John 15:6)

Not just says, "I believe," but *remains with Christ* in all he does.

Jesus will only call us a friend *if we do everything that He commands us to do.* (John 15:14)

> "For we are made partakers of Christ *if*, from the beginning *to the very end*, we hold steadfast to the True *covenant.*" (Hebrews 3:14)

In order to sit on one of the thrones in the Kingdom of God, we must "follow" Jesus...not just *say* we believe in Him, but *"follow"* Him. That is made clear in Matthew 19:28.

Proof that "once saved, always saved" is a false teaching couldn't be more clearly shown than in the case of Judas: one of Jesus' Apostles, chosen by Jesus Himself, yet he fell away…betraying Jesus with a kiss (Mark 14:44). Did Judas's original faith grant him salvation that could never be lost? Not according to Mark 14:21. Jesus said that it would have been better for the man who betrayed him if he had never been born. Although chosen by Jesus, Himself, to be one of His disciples, Judas sold his salvation for 30 pieces of silver.

But we have another problem. Can we believe in Jesus if we don't really know who He is? This leads to the *fourth* and most important thing we get from John 3:16: the declaration of who Jesus is. God so loved the world that He sent *His only begotten Son.*

The One that God sent was His *begotten* Son.

Most of Christendom does not even know who Jesus is, though the Bible tells us hundreds of times. It tells us that He is God's Son, and that God sent Him so that if we believe in Him, we can have everlasting life.

It does not say that He, God, came down in the form of His Son. It tells us that this Son was *begotten*…not made as Adam had been made…but begotten by God's Spirit…begotten by God's power…and born of a woman. It tells us that Jesus was flesh and blood.

John 3:6 makes it clear that one born of flesh *is* flesh, so we know that Jesus was a mortal, able to sin and able to die…just as you and I…born with a sinful nature just as all mortal men are born…that He was flesh and blood. (Romans 8:3)

John, in his second letter, tells us that one who does not acknowledge that Jesus *came in the flesh*, is an anti-Christ. If one believes that Jesus is God, he cannot believe that Jesus was sinful flesh, as we've been assured that He was.

John 3:16 describes the offer of salvation which is conditional upon belief in Jesus, *the man*. We have to know who He is or we cannot believe in Him.

Trinitarians are taught that Jesus and God are the same…two persons but one God. That They (and the Holy Spirit…which they believe to be the third God-person of the Trinity) are all three *omnipotent*...all powerful. That they are all three *omniscient*…all knowing. That they are all three *omnipresent*…everywhere at all times. Co-equal.

It is not difficult to see from the scriptures that this is not so, and will be discussed thoroughly in the next chapter. Jesus dwelt among the Apostles, who saw and touched Him and ate with Him and prayed with Him. Yet John 1:18 says no man has seen God. Doesn't that tell us that Jesus is *NOT* God?

> *If we believe in any Jesus other than the Jesus that God sent, we cannot expect to receive everlasting life*. We cannot expect to avoid the death passed on to us by Adam. (2 Corinthians 11:4, 13)

If we read it carefully and search out the Scriptures that support it, John 3:16 tells us all we need to know about salvation.

What is wrong with believing that Jesus is God? Nothing…except that it is a lie! Believing a lie will not give you entrance into God's Kingdom.

> "Let him who reads understand." (Mark 13:14)

Let us assume that you have taken out your Bibles; that you have searched for, and understand, the *Truth*; that you have accepted Jesus as your Savior; have repented of your sins; and have been baptized into His name. Are you now saved, unconditionally and without further requirements? Those teaching you, assure you that now, "No man can separate you from God." But the scripture they are relying on is Romans 8:35-39, and it does not stop at that declaration. If you will go to your Bible, you will see that a very important portion of that scripture has been omitted. It should read:

> "No one can separate us from the love of God
> *which is in Jesus Christ our Lord."*

Those who do not believe in Jesus...the Jesus of the Bible...cannot expect that they are included in those who are loved by God sufficiently to be saved without meeting the conditions set forth in the Scriptures. The love of God "which is in Jesus Christ," presupposes an acceptance of Jesus sufficient that we receive this love from which we cannot be separated.

Most assuredly, no *man* can snatch you from the hand of your Savior. But that does not say that you, yourself, cannot lose (or give up) the salvation you believe you have secured for yourself.

Once you let it be known that you have found the Truth and know who Jesus is, there will be many who will be happy to assist you in losing that faith. In fact, you will find it difficult to find a church that will accept you as a member when you do not accept the lie of the Trinity.

In Mark 13:13, Jesus, Himself, warns that, "You will be *hated* by all for My names sake..."

Scripture warns us that salvation does not result from an initial and verbal acceptance. Yes, it is a gift, but, it must be remembered, a gift cannot be forced upon you. You are free to accept it, reject it, refuse it, or, even after acceptance, to return it. And it can be reclaimed by the giver if the recipient does not adhere to the conditions of the gift.

We do not receive salvation as an *unconditional* gift from God. The very offer is conditional on our belief in His Son. (John 3:16) and we are told that "we are left to work out our own salvation with fear and trembling." (Philippians 2:12)

Salvation results from living the "*new life*" which begins when we are "*born again*" in Christ at our baptism. The passage in Mark 13:13 continues by letting us know that:

> "...But he that endures *to the end* shall be saved."
>
> "Be *faithful until death* and I will give you the crown of life," (Revelations 2:10) but "*If your heart turns away...you shall surely perish.*" (Deuteronomy 30:17,18)

Endurance in the faith that you know and express at the time of your baptism is one of the conditions imposed upon the *True* Christian.

> "If we *endure*, we shall also reign with Him." (2 Timothy 2:12*)* but

> "If we sin *willfully* after we have received the knowledge of the Truth, there no longer remains a sacrifice for sins..." (Hebrews10:26)

Jesus died as a sacrifice for our sins and that sacrifice will not remain if we deliberately go against the commandments of Jesus Christ.

> "Jesus said…'No one, having put his hand to the plow and looking back is fit for the kingdom of God.'" (Luke 9:62)

This "looking back" is an example of accepting the gift of salvation and returning it to the giver, telling us that anyone who has accepted Christ, then turns away, is not fit for God's kingdom.

Of course we will sin after acceptance of our Lord, since sin is the mere doing, saying or thinking of *anything* that is not pleasing to God. However, we must not sin *willfully,* and we must repent and ask for forgiveness when we do sin. We must live by faith.

> "The just shall live by faith; but *if anyone draws back*, my soul has no pleasure in him." (Hebrews 10:38)

> "...if you *continue* in His goodness…otherwise *you will be cut off."* (Romans 11:22)

There are many warnings about the danger of falling away…of losing the salvation we thought we had attained.

> "Unless a man *remains* with me, he will be cast outside like a branch which is withered, which they pick up and throw into the fire to be burned." (destroyed). (John 15:6)

> "A man who *wanders from the way* of understanding will rest in the assembly of the dead." (Proverbs 21:16)

We cannot just know the Truth about who Jesus is and express a desire to be saved. We must live our lives in obedience to His commandments. He promises salvation "to all them who *obey* Him." (Hebrews 5:9)

One of those commandments to be obeyed is to be baptized. A whole chapter will be devoted to baptism, but we know that it is a requirement because the Bible tells us so.

> "He who believes *and is baptized* will be saved." (Mark 16:16)

There is not a Christian church in the world that will not stress the fact that works (doing good) will *not* buy you a ticket into the Kingdom. But, unlike the lies that are perpetrated from the leaders of the churches of all denominations, works *are* essential.

> "Man is justified by *works* and *not by faith alone.*" (James 2:24)

If man has the type and quality of faith that would earn for him salvation...entry into God's Kingdom...that faith will result in good works.

> "Faith, by itself, *if it does not have works, is dead.*" (James 2:17).

No, salvation is not unconditional. More is expected of us than a knowledge of Jesus; more than an understanding of the Gospel (the Good News of the Kingdom of God); more than a *statement* of acceptance of Him as our Savior; more than just being baptized. Jesus expects His believers to do good works *in His name* and *for His sake*, and our faith is *measured by those works.*

> "The just shall live by faith; but *if anyone draws back*, I have no pleasure in him." (Hebrews 10:38)

If we go to 2 Peter 2:20-22, it becomes clear that the promise "Once saved always saved," that is taught from the pulpit, is a false one. It assures us, in no uncertain terms, that if one accepts Christ and then turns away, "*it would have been better for them not to have known the way of righteousness, than having known it to turn from the holy commandment delivered to them.*" It compares such turning away to a dog returning to it's own vomit and a sow, having washed, going back to wallowing in the mire.

What must I do to be saved? It is the One who bestows the gift that has the right to determine the conditions upon which that gift of salvation will be granted. The Scriptures make it clear that the conditions, or lack of them, preached from the pulpits of today are false.

THE LIE:
Jesus is God

How can we believe that Jesus is God when the first of all the commandments is, *"The Lord our God is One Lord*"?

At the beginning of the New Testament we are told that it is "*The book of the genealogy of Jesus Christ, the son of David, the son of Abraham.*" Then the descendants of Abraham are listed through David and on to Joseph, the husband of Mary, "*of whom was born Jesus, who is called Christ.*" (Matthew 1:1-16) Mary, too, was of the line of David. God had promised to bring forth the Savior through the line of David. Is it not absurd to believe that *God* came through the line of David, knowing that God is eternal?

Through the power of His Spirit... "the power of the Highest"...God begot Jesus, through the virgin Mary. (Luke 1:35)

From His mother, Mary, Jesus derived the sinful nature common to mankind, (Romans 8:3) including the ability to be tempted in all things as any other man, thus the ability to sin. (Hebrews 4:15)

From His Father, God, He inherited latent spiritual proclivities that strengthened Him to conquer the flesh...the sinful nature...and to develop divine characteristics. (1 John 3:9)

If you had never heard a sermon on the Bible; if you had never had a teacher give you a lesson on the Bible; if you had never heard anyone's opinion of what was in the Bible; you could read the Bible from cover to cover and never find anything that would suggest to you that God was three persons…a Trinity…or that Jesus is God. It isn't there!

If you believe that Jesus is God, then you have to believe that *God* was born of a human mother. God certainly was not born of a woman. In fact, God was never born at all, but has always been. Jesus is the Son of God…not God the Son. *"God the Son" is a phrase that never appears in the Bible.*

Dr. Charles Stanley, an internationally known Baptist TV preacher and teacher from Atlanta, Georgia, expressing the teachings of nearly all of Christendom, said, "If you *don't believe that Jesus is God,* then you might as well forget being saved."

Dr. Stanley continued by explaining that Jesus and God were the same…that there was no difference in them...that both knew everything (were *Omniscient*); both were everywhere at all times (were *Omnipresent*); and that both had unlimited power (were *Omnipotent*).

While Dr. Stanley did not mention the Holy Spirit in his discussion of these powers, we have to assume that this third "person" of the Three-in-One God in whom he believes…and of whom he teaches…also has these same powers. In this discussion, however, I'll concentrate primarily on God and His Son, Jesus, because Dr. Stanley did.

Instead of absorbing the messages given us by priests, preachers, teachers, and evangelists without question, we should be "going to the Scriptures to see if what they say is true," (Acts 17:11) because we are told in John 4:24, that we must worship in *Truth.*

I am going to give you, here, Scriptures that will prove that Jesus is *NOT* God. But I beg you not to take my word for it and I hope you will go to your Bibles and study all these verses and try to understand what they are telling you.

If Jesus is God, to whom did He have to "become obedient" (Phiiippians 2:8), from whom did He have to "learn obedience" (Hebrews 5:8), and what would there be for Him to learn if He were God Himself, who knew all things?

If Jesus is God, how could He possibly be "made a little lower than the angels"? (Hebrews 2:9) Could God be lower than the angels?

If Jesus is God, why did He have to be "made so much better than the angels"? (Hebrews 1:4) Wasn't God already better than the angels?

If Jesus is God, and knew everything already, why did He have to "increase in wisdom"? (Luke 2:52)

If Jesus is God, why would He have to be "*made* perfect"? (Hebrews 5:9) Wasn't He already perfect?

Revelations 5:12 tells us that Jesus had to be "slain to receive power and riches and wisdom and might and honor and glory and blessings." That says to me that Jesus could not have been God, because He did not have these attributes *until after his death* on the cross.

And God called Jesus his "servant." (Matthew 12:18) Does that sound like an equal?

If Jesus is God, why did God have to give Him commandments...tell Him what to say; why did Jesus say that He could "do nothing of Himself but what He seeth the Father do"? (John 7:16)

If Jesus is God, how could He be tempted? "God cannot be tempted..." (James 1:13) "but Jesus...hath suffered being tempted...in all points tempted like as we are." (Hebrews 2:18; 4:15)

If Jesus is God, coming into a sinful world, then the scriptures lie when they say that "God cannot dwell in the presence of sin." (Habakkuk 1:13)

If Jesus is God and equal to God, why would He say "My Father is greater than I"? (John 14:28)

We already know that Jesus was born of a virgin. If Jesus, God, and the Holy Spirit are three persons (but One God), why is Jesus not called the Son of God the Holy Spirit rather than the Son of God the Father? The Bible says, "She (Mary) was found with child of the Holy Spirit...that which is conceived in her is of the Holy Spirit."(Matthew 1:18-20)

The angel that came to Mary as God's agent told her that the Power of God (the Holy Spirit) would rest upon her and that "the one who is to be born of you is Holy and He will be called the *Son of God,"... not* God the Son. (Luke 1:35) The Holy Spirit is not a separate being, but the Power of God. (Luke 1:35)

If Jesus *is* God, isn't it absurd to say that He is "a mediator between us and God"? (1 Timothy 2:5)

If Jesus is God, would He say "I am the offspring of David"? (Revelations 22:16) "Remember Jesus Christ who rose from the dead, He who was *a descendant from David...*" (2 Timothy 2:8) I can't imagine God being an offspring of David. Is it possible that God could be a descendant of David?

If Jesus is God, does that mean that God is from the body (a descendant) of Abraham? (Genesis 15:4)

If Jesus is God, why could He not speak for Himself? Why did He say "...the Father who sent Me, He commanded Me what to say and what to speak." (John 12:49).

If Jesus is God, how can He be an heir of Himself...and how can *we* be "*heirs with Christ*" unless Christ is the heir and Son of God? (Romans 8:17)

If Jesus is God, then the promises of being brethren of Christ means that we will be brethren of God rather than God's children. (Hebrews 2:11)

If Jesus is God, we *don't* have the high Priest we were *promised*, who can appear on our behalf before God! (Hebrews 9:24; 4:14)

If Jesus is a part of a Triune God, why (in Revelations 21:22) does John say, "I saw no temple in it, for the Lord God Almighty *and* the Lamb (Jesus) *are* it's temple." Where is the Holy Spirit...the Third Person of the Trinity?

If Jesus is God, why does John say that Jesus doesn't sin because "God's *seed* is in Him...He has been born *of* God"...born *of* God, not born *as* God. (1 John 3:9)

If Jesus is God, how can He *belong* to God? "And you are Christ's (in writing to the church at Corinth) and Christ is God's."(1 Corinthians 3:23)

In Isaiah 43:10, God tells us that "*Before Me, there was no God created, neither shall there be after Me.*" That says to me that there was no pre-existent "God" before the One God, and there would be no other God after Him. That removed the title of "God the Son" from Jesus, and leaves Him to be just who both He and God said He was...the only *begotten* Son of God, His Father. (John 3:16)

Referring to Jesus, Hebrews 1:4 states: "having become so much better than the angels, as He has *by inheritance* obtained a more excellent name than they." Jesus had to *become* better than the angels? Could He, then, be God? He *inherited* His more excellent name...He did not possess it as God.

If Jesus is God, how can there be two separate wills in One being? "I seek not Mine own will, but the will of the Father..." (John 5:30) "I came, not to do My will, but the will of Him who sent Me." (John 6:38) "Not My will but Thine be done." (Luke 22:42) Even if there were One God but three Persons, wouldn't they *all* have the same will?

Jesus died! If Jesus is God, then God can die...meaning that God is corruptible...that God is mortal man. Yet we know that the Scriptures tell us that God is *incorruptible*...that God is *not a man.* (Hosea 11:9) How far astray Christendom has come from the Truth of the Bible.

Jesus dwelt among the Apostles who saw and touched and ate and prayed with Him and beheld His glory, (John 1:14) yet John 1:18 says "No man hath seen God at any time." Doesn't this tell us that Jesus *cannot be God*?

While God gave to His Son, Jesus, power and authority, He withheld information that only He, God, would know.

> "But concerning that day and that hour (when Christ would return) no man knows, not even the angels of heaven, *neither the Son,* but *only the Father.*" (Mark 13:32)

These are words of Jesus, Himself. Can't we believe Him when He tells us that He isn't omniscient?

If Jesus is God, why did He need to be "highly exalted" (and who exalted Him)? (Philippians 2:9)

"We are sons of God through our brotherhood with Christ." (Galatians 3:26-27) If we become sons of God by being a brother with Christ, then Christ must be the Son of God. We are God's sons and daughters (Galatians 4:6-7) and we can only attain that status by becoming brothers and sisters of Christ. If Christ is God, we become brothers and sisters of God. Nothing in the Scriptures even hints at such an absurdity.

"Every prophesy which declares that Jesus Christ is come in the flesh is from God." (1 John 4:2) We know that Jesus Christ came in the flesh...(He was born of a woman). But the verse doesn't tell us that this *flesh* came from God, it tells us that the *prophesy* came from God.

Jesus was, and is, the *revelation* of God:
(Revelation: An act of revealing or communicating divine Truth. God's disclosure of His will to man; something that contains or serves to communicate.) Jesus was the agent of God to disclose to man, God's Truth. (Acts 17:31)

Jesus was, and is, the *manifestation* of God:
(Manifestation: Something that manifests or constitutes an expression of *something else.*) Jesus was sent to *explain* God...not to *be* God. (Romans 16:26)

Jesus is *NOT* the *incarnation* of God:
(Incarnation: an embodiment of a Deity in some earthly form or being.) Incarnation is a word that *never appears in the Bible...*only in the teachings of the Roman Catholic Church, beginning in the 3rd century after Christ, and adopted by other denominations thereafter.

In its Athanasian Creed, the early Roman Church declared that Jesus was "perfect" from birth. But that is not what the Bible tells us. Hebrews 5:9 tells us that "He (Jesus) was a *good* Son...and that He *grew* to be perfect." If Jesus had been God, He would have been perfect from His birth, but we are told that He wasn't perfect...that He was good; that he was tempted as we are; and that He only became perfect when He died without having sinned. If He had been God, then living His life without sin would have entailed no special accomplishment...would have accomplished nothing. God cannot sin.

Christ's words teach us that eternal salvation is conditional upon a person worshiping God in *TRUTH.* (John 4:24) I am amazed at the lengths to which those, entrusted with the Truth to teach, will go to try to prove the false doctrine of the Trinity. On a Larry King Live-CNN television show, Larry was interviewing a Baptist minister, a Rabbi, and a Catholic priest on the subject of who Jesus is. As many may know, in addition to the expressions of opinions given by the guests, there is a call-in portion. In this particular instance, a woman called to say that she had been baptized in the name of Jesus Christ. Did she need, she asked, to be re-baptized in the name of the Trinity in order to go to heaven?

The Catholic priest fielded this question and, after referring her to Acts 19:2-5, proceeded to recite what he implied was this Scriptural verse, saying:

> "A man named Apollos, who worked in Corinth, and he was baptized in the name of Jesus, and he had to be corrected so it was only after his correction that he realized that he needed to be baptized in the name of the Trinity."

Whoooo!

That lady probably accepted that as truth, though the Bible tells us to listen to the teachers... but to go to the Scriptures and search to see if what they say is the Truth. (Acts 17:11; John 5:39) I will tell you what that Scripture says, though I beg you to go to your Bible and search it out for yourselves.

Apollos told Paul that his life had not changed since his baptism, that he had not received the Holy Spirit. When

> Paul asked him by what baptism he had been baptized, he responded "By the baptism of *John*" (Not *Jesus* as the Priest expounded).
>
> Paul explained that John baptized the baptism of repentance, but that the baptism of salvation was Jesus Christ, and that only through baptism into *Jesus* could he be born again. So, understanding this, Apollos was *"baptized in the name of our Lord, Jesus Christ"* (*not the Trinity,* as the Priest falsely led her to believe).

The caller could have gone to her Bible and learned that she had been deceived. I wonder if she did, or whether she just accepted the lie as Truth…as most of Christendom does?

The Priest cannot be excused as having misinterpreted the Scripture. The Scripture is perfectly clear. He *lied* to support a doctrine that is not supportable by Scripture….lied to support the false doctrines Jesus warned against.

I wish that the priest's deception had been the only wrongful thing "done" to Truth on this Larry King program, but our Baptist minister friend added to the deception.

> He said, rightfully, when asked who Jesus was:
>
> "it is in the Scripture that is the evidence for Jesus; it is the authority whereby we know who Jesus was and what He did; what He said. It is interesting that the question you asked tonight was specifically asked by the Lord Himself. He took His disciples off to the region of Caesarea Philippi and in Matthew 16, He asked them first 'Who do others say that I am,' then He turned to his own disciples and He said, 'And who do *you* say I am?' And Simon Peter said 'Thou art the Christ, the *Son of the living God!*' and Jesus said 'That's right.'"

If he had stopped there, one could have had a great deal of respect for him, but he continued by corrupting the Scripture thusly:

> "That is the confession of the true church through all the ages, that Jesus Christ is very God of every Man and the *incarnation* of very God of very God, fully God and fully Man...."

Waaaait a minute!

Jesus said all of that when he confirmed his disciples' statement that He was "the Christ, the Son of the living God"?

Please go back and read Matthew 16:15-17.

The Rabbi on the program made it clear that the reason few Jews accept Jesus is because Jews cannot accept the idea of a triune God. Neither should anyone hoping to be in God's eternal Kingdom.

On another Larry King show, a woman minister complained that some pastors were more interested in teaching *True doctrine* than in preaching what the people want to hear. Paul, in his second letter to Timothy (in chapter 4, verse 3) warned, even then, that the time would come when people would not endure sound doctrine...would not put up with the Truth...but would heap upon themselves teachers that would teach what their itching ears wanted to hear.

I would like to suggest that this woman minister should have no fear that "some pastors are more interested in teaching True doctrine than in preaching what the people want to hear." Unfortunately, pastors with a concern for the True doctrine are few and far between...in spite of the fact that our salvation is contingent upon believing the *Truth.* (John 4:24)

At a Bible study session hosted by Tim Newman, a young Calvary Chapel minister in Kailua, Hawaii, the pastor was reading the passage in John, Chapter 11, in which it is related that Jesus asked Martha whether she believed that those who believed in Him would never die. All those present in the study group dropped their eyes to their Bibles to follow along as Reverend Newman read Martha's response:

> "Yes my Lord, I do believe that you are the Christ, the Son of God, who is to come to this world."

The passage stopped there, but Pastor Newman kept on without the slightest hesitation, as though he were still reading:

> "I believe you are God incarnate, the incarnate God..."

I glanced around the room and saw that not a soul (other than I) lifted their eyes from their Bibles. They followed along just as though that last sentence had been written in their own Bibles; as though the words that had been read by their pastor actually appeared on the pages of their Bibles. It was not there. But, like so much of Christendom, it was accepted as though it had been, thus perpetuating the lie that Jesus is God.

The most compelling passages of Scripture to prove that Jesus is *not* God are:

> Isaiah 46:9: "For *I am God* and *there is no Other."* (*God* the Son is another God; *God* the Holy Spirit is another God; but *God* said, "there is *no Other.*")

> Mark 13:32: When Jesus was asked when the end times would come, He responded, "...of that day and hour no one knows, not even the angels in heaven, *nor the Son, but only the Father."* Does He sound like an Omniscient (all knowing) God?

> 1 Corinthians 15:24, 28: "Then comes the end, when He (Jesus) delivers the kingdom to God the Father...when all things are made subject to Him (God)...then *the Son Himself will also be subject to Him (God)."*

At the time of His greatest triumph...when He had succeeded in removing all sin from the world...Jesus turns everything over to God, and He Himself becomes subject to God. It is clearly obvious that He is not co-equal with His Father. He is *not* God. He is who He said He was. He is who God said He was. He is God's Son.

> Romans 1:22-23: This, to me, explains in greatest detail what the worship of Jesus as God really is. "While they thought within themselves that they were wise, they became fools, and they have changed the glory of the *incorruptible* God for an image made in the likeness of *corruptible* man…."

The Bible tells us that God is incorruptible…that He is eternal…that He is *not man* (Numbers 23:19; Hosea 11:9) and John 10:33; 1 Corinthians 15:21 and 1 Timothy 2:5 tell us that Jesus was "*only* a man." How can One who is *only* a man and one who is *not* a man, be One?

To believe that Jesus is God, is to drag the incorruptible God down and to turn Him into the corruptible man which Jesus was, and to worship Him as God. Worshiping the created rather than the Creator. This, God called idol worship, and *"idolatry, God will not forgive."* (Deuteronomy 29:18)

Further, Ephesians 5:5 tells us that no one who serves idols has any inheritance in the kingdom of Christ and of God.

God told us that Jesus was His beloved Son. Why can't we believe Him?

Encyclopedia Britannica says about the Trinity:
"Fundamental to the Old testament and the New, is the monotheistic credo summarized in Deuteronomy 6:4: 'Hear O Israel, the Lord our God is One Lord.' *Neither Jesus nor His early followers intended anything they said about their new revelation to contradict that credo.* Nevertheless, the awareness of these implications did not spring into the Christian consciousness all at once but *developed over several centuries and through many controversies*. The propositions constitutive of the dogma of the Trinity were not drawn directly from the New Testament and could not be expressed in New Testament terms. These were the products of reason, speculating on a revelation to faith. *They were only formed* through centuries of effort, only elaborated *by the aid of the conceptions and formulated in the terms of Greek and Roman metaphysics.*" (Emphasis provided)

Going to the Encyclopedia Americana:
Here we're told more about the Trinity. "It is held that although the doctrine is beyond the grasp of human reason, it is, like many of the formulations of

physical science, not contrary to reason, and may be apprehended (though it may not be comprehended) by the human mind." (Emphasis provided)

Does that make the Trinity perfectly clear to everyone?

There have been many Trinities throughout the ages, but never in the Hebrew religion and never associated or related to Judaism. The word "Trinity" *never appears in the Bible.*

An idol was found in the Temple on Elephanta Island, Bombay, which had three heads, the pagan form of the Trinity as expressed in the mythology of Hinduism. The three gods, Bhairava, the god of Destruction; Brahma, the Creator; and Vishnu, the Preserver, are treated as one.

Ecclesiastical history shows how the pagan doctrine of the Trinity was gradually superimposed upon the Truth until it completely obscured it, fulfilling Paul's warning of 2 Timothy 4:3, which says:

> "For the time will come when men will not listen to sound doctrine; but they will add for themselves extra teachers according to their desires, being lured by enticing words."

I remind you of the woman minister who complained that some preferred True doctrine rather than what people wanted to hear. Clearly, the warning of 2 Timothy 4:3 is alive and well in today's churches.

If Jesus is *NOT* God, then how did this Trinity doctrine come into being?

The decline of the early church was gradual:

120 A. D., the Apostles Creed said simply, "I believe in God the Father Almighty, and in Jesus Christ, His Son."

150 A. D. Justin Martyr begins to corrupt Christianity with the philosophy of the Greeks.

170 A. D. The word *Trias* first occurs in Christian literature.

200 A. D. The word *Trinitas* is first used by Tertuallian.

260 A. D. Sabellius teaches: Father, Son, and Holy Spirit are three names for the same God.

300 A. D. No Trinitarian forms of prayer yet known to the church.

310 A. D. Lactantius (orthodox teacher) writes: *"Christ never* calls himself God."

325 A. D. The Nicene Council introduces, *for the first time*, the idea of a pre-existent Christ and agrees to call Christ "God of God, the God of very God" and develops the Nicene Creed, as follows:

"We believe in one God, the Father Almighty, Creator of all things visible and invisible, and in one Lord Jesus Christ, the only begotten of the Father, that is the substance of the father, through whom all was made that is in heaven and on earth, and became flesh, became man, suffered and rose on the third day, is ascended to heaven and will come to judge the living and the dead. And in the Holy Spirit, the Lord and giver of life, who proceeds from the Father, and with the Father and Son together is worshiped and glorified, who spake by the prophets. We believe in one Holy Catholic and Apostolic Church; we acknowledge one baptism for the forgiveness of sins; we look for the resurrection of the dead; and the life of the world to come. Amen."

350 A. D. Great conflicts in the church about the doctrine of the Trinity.

370 A. D. The Doxology, "Glory to the Father, to the Son and to the Holy Ghost," is composed and complained of as a novelty.

381 A. D. The Council of Constantinople gives the finishing touch to the doctrine of "three persons in one God," and publishes the Athanasian Creed.

As has been shown, it wasn't until 381 A. D. that the Athanasian Creed was put into place...long after the Apostles were dead. Pagans attempted to (and did) influence the Christian religion, especially after the death of the Apostles.

When the Emperor Constantine had a dream in which he saw a cross, he declared that he had become a Christian (though many doubt that he ever did) and ordered that the Christian religion be the religion of all the land...of all the world that was known at that time. Everyone was forbidden to practice any other religion.

The Christians worshiped One God. The Pagans worshiped idols and multi-gods, and it was very difficult to bring them into the Christian influence. Finally, Constantine, tired of all the bloodshed over the name of Jesus, wanted peace between the two warring groups, ordered the church convene a conference and to come up with a doctrine that *all* could embrace.

The silver craftsmen of that day were no different than those of Paul's day (Acts 19:23-24,38) in that they feared the worship of One God would destroy their livelihoods. They crafted silver idols of their many gods, selling them at great profit. Having to accept Christianity...the worship of one God...would, they knew, destroy all that. Yet the Christian church had been ordered to come up with a doctrine that would be acceptable to everyone, and so the birth of the corruption-of-faith that always accompanies compromise-in-faith. The Roman church created it's own multi-God...the Trinity... "invented" so that the pagans needed only to rename their gods. The Athanasian Creed was the result. It stated:

"Whoever would be saved needeth before all things to hold fast to the Catholic faith. Which faith except a man keep whole and undefiled without doubt, he will perish eternally. Now the Catholic faith is this, that we worship one God in Trinity and Trinity in Unity; neither confusing the persons nor dividing the substance, for there is one person of the Father, another of the Son, and another of the Holy Ghost. But the Godhead of the Father, and of the Son and of the Holy Ghost is all one, the glory equal, the majesty co-eternal, such as the Father is, such is the Son, and such is the Holy Ghost; The Father uncreated, the Son uncreated, the Holy Ghost uncreated; the Father infinite, the Son infinite, the Holy

Ghost infinite; the Father eternal, the Son eternal, the Holy Ghost eternal; yet there are not three eternals, but one eternal; as also there are not three uncreated, not three infinites, but one infinite and one uncreated. So likewise the Father is almighty, the Son almighty, the Holy Ghost almighty; and yet there are not three almighties, but one almighty. So the Father is God, the Son God, the Holy Ghost God; and yet there are not three gods but one God. So the Father is Lord, the Son Lord, the Holy Ghost Lord; and yet there are not three Lords, but one Lord. For like as we are compelled by the Christian verity to confess each person by himself to be both God and Lord; so we are forbidden by the Catholic religion to speak of three gods or three lords. The Father is made of none, nor created, nor begotten. The Son is of the Father alone; not made, not created, but begotten. The Holy Ghost is of the Father alone; not made, nor created, nor begotten, but proceeding.

There is, therefore, one Father, not three Fathers; one Son, not three Sons; one Holy Ghost, not three Holy Ghosts. And in this Trinity there is no one before or after, no greater or less; but all three persons are co-eternal together, and co-equal. So that in all ways, as is aforesaid, both the Trinity is to be worshiped in Unity, and the Unity in Trinity. He that therefore would be saved, let him think thus of the Trinity. Furthermore, it is necessary to eternal salvation, that he also believe faithfully the incarnation of our Lord Jesus Christ. Now the right faith is that we believe and confess that our Lord Jesus Christ, the Son of God, is both God and man. He is God, of the substance of the Father, begotten before worlds; and He is man of the substance of His mother, born in the world; perfect man, of reasoning soul and human flesh subsisting; equal to the Father as touching His Godhead; less than the Father as touching His manhood. Who, although He be God and man, yet He is not two, but is one Christ; one, however, not by conversion of His Godhead into flesh, but by taking of manhood into God; one altogether; not by confusion of the substance, but by unity of person. For as reasoning soul and flesh is one man, so God the man is one Christ, Who suffered for our salvation, descended into hell, rose again from the dead, ascended into heaven, sat down at the right hand of the Father, from whence He shall come to judge the quick and the dead. At whose coming all men will rise again with their bodies, and shall give account for their deeds. And they that have done good will go into life eternal; they that have done evil into eternal fire. This is the Catholic faith, which except a man do faithfully and steadfastly believe, he cannot be saved."

383 A. D. The Emperor Tehodosius threatens to punish all who will not believe in and worship the Trinity.

519 A. D. This Doxology is ordered to be sung in all Christian Churches

669 A. D. The clergy commanded to commit to memory the Athanasian Creed incorporating the doctrine of the Trinity.

826 A. D. Bishop Basil orders the clergy to recite every Sunday.

It took over 300 years after Christ, for the doctrine of the Trinity to obscure the Truth of who Jesus really was and is. But it took over another *one thousand years* for the Catholic (the Universal) church to manage to have wording inserted into 1 John 5:7 and 8 that would appear to prove the Three-in-One doctrine it taught and demanded to be believed.

Until the 15th century, that passage read thusly:
"For there are three that bear witness, the Spirit, the water, and the blood; and these three agree as one."

At the insistence of the Church, other language was inserted and recent Bibles carry the amended version, i.e.:

"For there are three that bear witness (*in heaven*: *the Father,* the Word and the Holy Spirit; and these three are one. And *there are three who bear witness on earth;)* the Spirit, the water, and the blood; and these three agree as one."

This Scripture (which is nowhere to be found in the ancient documents from which the translations were developed) is the only verse in the entire Bible to "prove" the Trinity. In spite of Christ's warning, in Revelation 22:19 of great plagues to anyone adding to His words, this addition was inserted *more than 1500 years after Christ's death.*

This man-inspired addition was a late attempt to prove a doctrine that is otherwise unsupportable by Scripture.

Having created the Trinity more than 300 years after Christ's death, the so-called Christian church, more than 1200 years later, invented the Scripture to support its apostate creation.

Salvation depends on belief in Jesus Christ. We cannot believe in Him if we do not know who He is, and He is *not* God, but God's begotten Son.

For over 200 years after Christ, the Creed (Statement of Belief) of the Christians was:

> "I believe in God, the Father Almighty, creator of heaven and earth, and in Jesus Christ His Son, our Lord, who was conceived by the Holy Spirit, born from the Virgin Mary, suffered under Pontius Pilate, was crucified, dead and buried, ascended into the heavens, sits on the right hand of God the Father Almighty, then will come to judge the living and the dead. I believe in the Holy Spirit, the holy Catholic (Universal) Church, the communion of saints, the remission of sins, the resurrection of the flesh, and eternal life."

This is still the creed of some non-Trinitarians...of whom there are few. But another 125 years later, the Nicene creed added another man-inspired doctrine...the idea of the pre-existence of Christ. (To be covered in a later chapter.)

"God is not the author of confusion." (1 Corinthians 14:33) Read the Athanasian Creed again, and tell me you *understand* what it says.

> "Unless you utter words easy to *understand,* how will it be known what is spoken, for you will be speaking into the air." (1 Corinthians 14:9)

If you can *understand* this Trinitarian Creed which was developed hundreds of years after Christ's death, you are more perceptive than I. Apparently I am not the only one who finds the doctrine absurd. Let me quote a few others who (though they accept it) also find it less than understandable.

Dr. W. R. Matthews, Dean of St. Paul's: "It must be admitted by everyone who has the rudiment of an historical sense that the doctrine of the Trinity, as a doctrine, *formed no part of the original message.* St. Paul knew it not and would have been unable to understand the meaning of the terms used in the theological formula on which the church ultimately agreed." (Emphasis provided)

Bishop Smaldridge (A Catholic himself): "It must be owned, that the doctrine of the Trinity as it is proposed in our articles, our liturgy, our creeds, *is not in so many words taught us in the Holy Scriptures.* What we profess in our prayers, we nowhere read in the Scriptures..." (Emphasis provided)

James Hughes – Roman Catholic Priest: "My belief in the Trinity is based on the authority of the Church; no other authority is sufficient. I will now show from reason that the *Athanasian Creed and the Scripture are opposed to one another*. The doctrine of the Trinity is this: There is one God in three persons, Father, Son, and Holy Ghost. The Father is God, the Son is God, and the Holy Ghost is God. Mind, the Father is one person, the Son is one person, and the Holy Ghost is another person. Now according to every principal of mathematics, arithmetic, human wisdom and policy, there must be three Gods; for no one would say that there are three persons and three Gods, and yet only one God. The Athanasian Creed gives the universal opinion of the Church, that the Father is uncreated, the Son is uncreated, and the Holy Ghost is uncreated...that they exist from all eternity. Now the Son was born of the Father and if born, must have been created. The Holy Ghost must have been created, he came from the Father and the Son, and if so, there must have been a time when they did not exist. If they did not exist they have been created: and therefore, to assert that they are eternal is absurd, and defies good sense. *Each has his distinct personality; each has his own essence. How can they be one Eternal?* How can they all be God. Absurd. The Athanasian Creed says that they are three persons and still be only one God? Absurd. Extravagant. This is rejected by every man following human reason. The Creed further says that our Lord Jesus Christ is the Son of God and of man, not by conversion of the Godhead into flesh but by taking the manhood of God. Now, I ask you, did the Divinity absorb the manhood? He could not be at the same time one person and two persons. *I have now proved the Trinity to be opposed to human reason."* (Emphasis provided)

Archbishop Secker, a Trinitarian, in his sermons: (referring to the doctrine of the Trinity) "Indeed let any proposition be delivered to us, as coming from God, or from man, *we can believe it no farther than we can understand it:* and therefore *if we do not understand it at all, we cannot believe it at all* - I mean explicitly; but only be persuaded, that it contains some truth or other, though we know not what. Again, were any doctrine laid down which we clearly saw to be self contradictory, or otherwise absurd, that could never be an object of our faith. For there is no possibility of admitting, upon any authority, a thing for true which we evidently perceive to be false. Nor would calling such a doctrine mysterious mend the matter in the least. For, indeed, there is no mystery in them, they are plain as any nature: *as plainly contrary to truth* as anything else is agreeable to it." (Emphasis provided)

Bishop Beverage: "The mysteries of the Gospel, which I am less able to conceive, I think myself the more obligated to believe; especially this mystery of mysteries, the Trinity in unity and unity in Trinity, which I am so far from being able to comprehend, or indeed to apprehend, that I cannot set myself seriously to think of it, or to screw up my thoughts a little concerning it, but I immediately lose myself in a trance or ecstasy: that God the Father should be one perfect God of Himself, God the Son one perfect unity of Himself, and God the Holy Ghost one perfect God of Himself; and yet that these three should be perfectly one; that the Father, Son and Holy Ghost, should be three and yet one; but one, and yet three! O Heart-amazing, thought-devouring, inconceivable mystery! Who cannot believe it to be true of the glorious Deity."

F. J. Wilkins, Professor of Theology, Baptist College of Victoria, Australia: "In the Old Testament, the Unity of God was clearly affirmed. The Jewish creed, repeated in every synagogue today, was 'Hear, O Israel, the Lord our God is one Lord' (Deuteronomy 6:4). *This was the faith of the first Christians*, so Paul writes 'There in one God and Father of all, who is above all and through all and in you all.' (Ephesians 4:6) *But gradually some additions or modifications of the creed were found necessary* ." (Emphasis provided)

In his statement, Mr. Wilkins implies that God had made a mistake in His proclamation, and that the theologians of the fourth century knew more about the matter than did Moses, Paul, Jesus Christ or God Himself!

Trinitarians describe, in their creed, Jesus as "Very God"...which means "of one."

Christ could not be Very God! Jesus was tempted (Hebrews 2:18) but God could not be tempted (James 1:13); Jesus died (Revelations 1:18) but God cannot die (1 Timothy 6:16); Jesus was seen by thousands...long and often...but God cannot be seen by man (1 Timothy 6:16); Jesus ascended to His Father and *His God.* (John 20:17); Even after His ascension, Jesus was still referred to as a man, but "God is *not a man*..." (Numbers 23:19)

The woman who asked Jesus to let her two sons sit at His right and left hand in the Kingdom, was told that this was not something that He could give, but for God to give. (Matthew 20:23) Does that sound like Jesus and God are the same, both all knowing; both with the same powers; and both everywhere at all times?

Trinitarians refer to the statement of Jesus that "I and my Father are one" as proof of the Trinity. This is a verse that, having already decided on the doctrine of the Trinity, the church found and embraced to prove their point. However, if you read further...and, in fact, search other translations, and passages in other books of the Bible...it has another meaning which becomes clear. In fact, the Lamsa translation reads, "I and my Father are *of one accord.*" When you consider that Jesus prayed that Paul and other disciples should be one with Him *as "I and my Father are one,"* the Lamsa translation has to be the correct meaning of the statement. Otherwise, we would have to believe that Jesus wanted the Apostles to become Him...and if He is God, then the Apostles also to become God. (John 17:11,22)

And God required that a man and wife be "one in flesh" (Matthew 19:5) but we know that this does not mean they are actually one person, but that they should be of one accord; one in purpose, objective and understanding...just as Jesus and God are of one accord; one in purpose and objective.

The Godhead is another word used by nearly all so-called Christians, who claim that the Godhead means the Trinity. "Godhead" means "the divine, the supreme being, the divine nature of God"....not "three in one." You need only do something as simple as opening your dictionary to find the definition of "Godhead," and it is *not* "three in one"...*not* Trinity.

Those who knew Jesus…those who walked and talked with Him, never thought that He was anything but what He said He was...the Son of God, with attributes of His Father, God, and attributes of His human mother, Mary.

Rarely are there arguments regarding whether or not "God the Holy Spirit," the so-called third person of the triune Gods, *is* God…or what effect not believing in *this* God would have on your salvation. This God is even left out of the hierarchy spelled out in 1 Corinthians 11:3, where we are told that man is head of his wife; that Christ is head of man; and that God is head of Christ. Where does the co-equal God-the-Holy Spirit fit into the picture?

Nowhere in the Bible can you find an incident of Jesus acting independently of God, nor of the Holy Spirit acting independently of either God or His Son, Jesus Christ. *It* (not he) is not represented in the Bible as the third "Person" of a Trinity, but as the power by which God achieves His ends in the world. Though the Holy Spirit is not "God the Holy Spirit," it is closer to *being* God than is Jesus, because the Holy Spirit is, in fact, God's power.

Through the power of his Spirit… "*the power of the Highest*"… God begot Jesus, through the virgin Mary. (Luke 1:35)

Results of believing in the Trinity:

It denies the Father of His glory. People think, when they say that Jesus is God, that they are elevating Jesus, when in fact they are bringing down the position of the Father, just as was described in Romans 1:22-23. They are worshiping the created rather than the Creator…something we have been warned against as prohibiting entrance into the Kingdom.

It minimizes the accomplishments of Jesus. If you think that Jesus is God, what did he accomplish by not sinning? God couldn't sin! If you recognize that Jesus had every trial that man has, even to being tempted, and still did *not* sin, then his accomplishments were magnificent. But if He were God, He couldn't be tempted, He couldn't sin. He accomplished nothing.

It distorts the atonement. You have to understand that Jesus was a man, and *only a man* (John 10:33, 1 Corinthians 15:21 and 1 Timothy 2:5) and that he died for the sins of many. Galatians says that he was made under the law that he might redeem those under the law. He had to be identified with those whom He was redeeming. He was one of us...cursed with mortality just as we are. He died to fulfill the will of God, that we might, by identifying with Him, have our sins forgiven. Our sins are paid for, in a sense, because it cost His life.

It denies the orderliness of the Word of God. When you think of how the Trinity was developed and the words used, it is obvious that it did not come from the Scriptures. Any verse originally used to support the Trinity, was an inferential verse...the doctrine is developed then verses are sought out that infer a support for that doctrine. You don't get the idea from the verse...you have to bring the verse out and say, "this verse helps me if I infer certain things."

But in doing this, you have to ignore the rest of the Scriptures. You have to ignore the fact that there are no contradictions in the Bible, and you fail to compare one Scripture with another, understanding the meaning of those Scriptures that must, by virtue of the difference, have a different meaning.

Later, the Church invented its own Scripture for the support it needed.

It denies YOU your salvation. We are told clearly that *if we believe any doctrine other than the one taught by the Apostles,* we are believing in myths and fables. To worship Jesus as God is idol worship and there is no place in God's Kingdom for idolaters.

If you ask people if they believe in the Trinity, most will say "Yes"....just as *you* might say "Yes." But if you are asked...and I ask you...to *explain* the Trinity, can you do it in any way other than to say that "God and Jesus and the Holy Spirit are three Persons but all One God"? And is there any way in the world that you can witness to anyone, explaining to them how that can be? Of course you could give them a copy of the Athanasian Creed... would that make it perfectly clear? I don't think so, and I don't believe that *you* think so!

> "If now you have *understanding* hear this; hearken to the voice of My words." (Job 34:16)...and God's words were "This is My beloved Son."

> Paul said,
> "In the church, I had rather speak five words with my *understanding*, that by my voice I might teach others also, than ten thousand words in an unknown tongue (something not understandable)..." (1 Corinthians 14:19)

The most important five words to be spoken are the words of God, Himself. "*This is my beloved Son.*"

The Gospel and Jesus Christ were meant to be *understood.* Jesus *wanted us to understand.* Several times He said "Hear Me, everyone, and *understand."* (Mark 7:14; Matthew 15:10) If people can't *understand* what you are trying to tell them, what good will it do them?

> "Will he who occupies the place of the uninformed say 'Amen' at your giving of thanks since he does not *understand* what you say?" (1 Corinthians 14:16)

> "Whoever hears the word of the Kingdom and does not *understand* it, the evil one (sin) snatches away the word which has been sown in his heart." (Matthew 13:19).

If you are relying on the "word" of the Trinity (which you cannot possibly understand) to give you a ticket into the Kingdom, be advised that the ticket will be snatched away, and you will find yourself outside, looking in...gnashing your teeth.

> "That which is sown upon good soil, this is he who hears my word and *understands* it..." (Matthew 13:23)

Jesus, Himself, taught by parables, and in the parable of the sower, He told us that "some seed fell on the roadside and was trodden under foot and the birds ate it." (Luke 8:5) He made it clear that "the seed is the word of God," (Luke 8:11) and that whoever hears the word of the Kingdom and *does not understand it*, the word will be snatched away by the evil one."(Matthew 13:19) Can you, who believe in the Trinity, understand it and preach it to others? Can you explain to an unbeliever how the only One God can be in the form of three persons? If not, Jesus assures you that you will be lost in sin and will not see the Kingdom.

If you cannot *understand* what is preached, then it certainly will not take root in your heart. The Trinity is not even understood by the church that developed it.

Jesus ordered His disciples to allow the false doctrines to be preached…to let *Him* take care of them when He returns…and at that time, He promised, He will gather them, bind them and burn them! (Matthew 13:24-30).

If you are relying on a church that teaches you these false doctrines, *find yourself another church!* A church that teaches the simple, easy to understand doctrine of the Apostles.

> "Consider what I say, and the Lord will give you *understanding* in all things." (2 Timothy 2:7)

Paul said that he prayed that the church would have *understanding* "so they might walk worthy of the Lord." (Colossians 1:9-10)

> "Then He opened their minds to *understand* the Scriptures." (Luke 24:45)

> "Wisdom is in the sight of him who has *understanding.*" (Proverbs 17:24)

> "Hear O you deaf! And *understand* and see, O you blind." (Isaiah 42:18).

> "...except you utter by the tongue words easy to *understand,* how shall it be known what you say? For you will be speaking into the air." (1 Corinthians 14:9)

You cannot possibly *understand* the doctrine of the Trinity which is set forth so completely in the Athanasian Creed…so how can you possibly share a faith in a doctrine *you cannot understand?* And if you cannot *understand,* how can you expect anyone to "say 'Amen' since he does not *understand* what you say?" (1 Corinthians 4:16)

> "For thou hast hid their hearts from *understanding;* therefore they shall exalt themselves in their deception. They shall go down to the bottom of sheol (the grave); they shall descend together into the dust." (Job 17:4,16)

The church that teaches the Trinity is deceiving itself and will die for it. Unfortunately, it will take with it all those who hear what they teach and do not *"search the scriptures to see if what they say is true."* (Acts 17:11, John 5:39)

> *"Give me understanding, and I shall live."* (Psalm 119:144)

A clear indication that if you do not have understanding, you will *not* live eternally. Eternal death will be your destiny.

Truth is "plain to him who *understands*." (Proverbs 8:6-9) The doctrine of the Apostles was "plain" and simple. The Roman church destroyed the Truth and it will pay the price. Other denominations which followed those same false doctrines, will likewise perish. But it is not just the Churches that will suffer...all those individuals who do not search out the Truth for themselves, will follow the Churches into eternal death.

We are assured that those who change the image of the incorruptible God for an image of corruptible man and worship Him as God; who change Truth for lies; who worship the created rather than the Creator...and many other wrongful things...all will be condemned by God and *"not only them, but those who associate with them."* (Romans 1:32)

> "...there shall be false teachers among you who shall bring in damnable heresies, even denying the Lord that bought them (with His blood) and bring upon themselves swift destruction." (2 Peter 2:1)

> "...sound doctrine" is *"understanding* and right." (Proverbs 8:14)

> "Forsake folly, and live; and go in the way of *understanding."* (Proverbs 9:6)

It is not too late to forsake the folly of the doctrine of the Trinity and to find your way to the Truth. Start with your Bible, it is the inspired word of God, and if you seek to learn Truth, He will lead you. Study with some group that knows the Truth.

Nobel Prize winning author Bertrand Russell wrote that the Christadelphians are the denomination that teaches doctrine most nearly to that of Jesus' Apostles.

> "The knowledge of the righteous is *understanding*." (Proverbs 9:10)

> "He who brings forth wisdom out of his lips shall beat with a rod him that lacks *understanding*." (Proverbs 10:13)...

> "*a man of understanding has wisdom*." (Proverbs.10:23)

> "Good *understanding* brings mercy." (Proverbs 13:15)

> "The vineyard of a man without *understanding* was all grown over with thorns..."(Proverbs 24:30-31)

People who have *no understanding* are called "foolish" (Jeremiah 5:21); power comes from *understanding* (Ezekiel 28:4); and we are told that we are to be mature in our *understanding* (1 Corinthians 14:20).

We were told, too, that even in Timothy's day (1 Timothy 1:6-7) some had already gone astray...had turned to foolish words... "*not understanding* what they speak" and we are warned against following their error. (2 Peter 3:17) Unfortunately, the Church as a whole, has not heeded the warning.

Jesus said "The first of all the commandments is 'Hear, O Israel, the Lord our God, the Lord is One and you shall love the Lord...with all your mind'." (Mark 12:31) How can you love with all of your *mind* what you can't *understand*?

Having seen all these verses (and there are many more the same or similar) that stress the importance of *understanding* the doctrine which we were instructed to preach, I would like to invite you to go back and read again *The Athanasian Creed* and tell me that you *understand* it.

> We were warned by Jesus that "after My departing shall grievous wolves enter in among you, not sparing the flock. Also *of your own selves* shall men arise, speaking perverse things, *to draw away disciples after them*." (Acts 20:29-30) "...there shall be false teachers among you...and bring upon themselves swift destruction." (2 Peter 2:1)

This so clearly prophesied what happened 300 years later...after Christ's death. The church developed the false doctrine of the Trinity, and they drew most of the followers of Jesus after them. These false teachers have assured themselves destruction...and unless those who believe in the Trinity turn away and find the True Jesus, they will follow in that everlasting destruction...everlasting separation from God.

Later, Paul, in his letter to Timothy, gave the same warning. He warned that the time would be coming when people would not tolerate sound and wholesome instruction, but having ears that itch to hear something pleasing and gratifying, will gather to themselves one teacher after another to a considerable number, chosen to satisfy their own liking and *to foster errors they hold*, and will turn aside from hearing the truth and wander off into *myth and man-made fiction*. (2 Timothy 4:3-4)

Isn't that exactly what has happened? Just a few hundred years after Jesus ascended into heaven, the Roman church, on instructions from Constantine, came up with the Athanasian Creed; declared that anyone who did not accept it as true would be damned; required the reciting of it by congregations at each service; later required the learning of it by heart. Even those who broke with the Catholic church, took with them this false doctrine.

Jesus and His disciples taught such a simple, easy to understand doctrine...that Jesus was the Son of God, that He came as a baby; born through the Power of God, to the virgin Mary; that He died for us; that He was raised by God from the dead; that He ascended into heaven to sit at the right hand of His Father; and that He would return to establish God's kingdom on earth.

> *"You were progressing well; who confused you that you should not obey Truth?"* (Galatians 5:7)

I ask the same question.

Where did we go wrong? The church led us into a false doctrine of "myth and man-made fiction" when it developed the doctrine of the Trinity….and most of Christendom has followed like sheep. It's time to get back to the Lamb of God, God's Son. What a pity that theologians make a mystery of the Godhead, confusing that which is plain and simple, turning it into something that is beyond the understanding that God requires.

The Trinity doctrine is one of those false teachings…a perverse thing…that will bring destruction upon many a would-be Christian. Even more punishment may befall the ones who teach the doctrine. The Catholic priests, themselves, find it an absurdity, but "believe" it because the Pope, who declares himself to be infallible, tells them they must.

But who was it that declared the Pope infallible? The Pope! Who decided that God's word needed modification? The Pope! But who said that all the terrible plagues described in Revelations would be added to anyone who did such a thing? Jesus! And He did not exclude the Pope. (Revelations 22:18)

Chuck Smith, one of the very popular Calvary Chapel pastors, in one of his sermons, said that "Elohim" is plural...three or more…"which," he said, "proves the Trinity." It didn't prove it to me, because I searched out the meaning from books that had *not* been written by Trinitarians, and I found, as I had suspected, that it isn't true. *Elohim* represents God in His relation to the world at large, as (1) Creator (2) providential ruler in the affairs of men, and (3) controlling the operations of nature. Yes, it says that He is plural…but plural in the nature of His *activities*…not in the nature of His *person.*

Jesus taught by parables, not by riddles. He used the stories to help His followers to *understand* spiritual things in an earthly setting. He did not hide what would have been the most profound teachings in some sort of riddle to be solved. Something so basic to a believer's faith as Jesus being God, would have been shouted from the housetops, were it true. In fact, the thing that was shouted was "*This is My beloved Son*, in whom I am well pleased." (2 Peter 1:17).

God said Jesus was His Son! Jesus said He was God's Son! Could there be any more substantial two witnesses to the Truth than God and Jesus? How can anyone who reads the Bible believe a bunch of bishops who, in order to appease pagans, came up with a Trinity myth and called it doctrine...how can a believer in Christ believe a doctrine developed some three or four hundred years *after* His death, over the word of God and Jesus, Themselves? And who can have faith in a church that manufactures Scripture to support its false doctrine because there is no such Scripture in God's word?

> In (Isaiah 43:10) God said:
> "Before Me there was no God formed. *Nor shall there be after me."*

God always was and always will be...nothing was before Him and nothing will be after Him.

> "...to you it was shown that you might know that the Lord Himself is God; *there is none other besides Him."* (Deuteronomy 4:35)

Jesus was neither God with Him at the time these words were spoken, nor God when He was born later. He simply is not God...but the Son that Both He and God said He was.

The acceptance of the doctrine of the Trinity by nearly all of Christendom, is a fulfillment of the prophesy that religious leaders would make the Word of God of non-effect through the traditions *they make for themselves.* (Mark 7:13; 2 Timothy 4:3)

Remember, Paul, in his letter to Timothy, warned that the time is coming when people will not tolerate sound and wholesome instruction, but having ears that itch to hear something pleasing and gratifying, will gather to themselves one teacher after another to a considerable number, chosen to satisfy their own liking and *to foster errors they hold*, and will turn aside from hearing the truth and wander off into *myth and man-made fiction*.(2Timothy 4:3-4)

Look at your own church. When someone is interviewed to be the new pastor, on what basis is he or she selected? Isn't the selection made on the basis of who gives the most interesting and appealing sermon? The one who is most likable; the most charismatic? The one who has the greatest following? Do they ever search the Scriptures to see whether what the applicant is teaching is the Truth?

What worries me is that many would-be Christians may miss their salvation because they did not "Believe that Jesus is the Son of God"...which is the condition set forth for salvation in John 3:16.

"A man who *wanders from the way of understanding* will rest in the assembly of the dead." (Proverbs 21:16) Apparently *no one understands the Trinity, not even the church that developed it.*

Christ is the image of the invisible God (Colossians 1:15)...so if the "image," then a *replica*, not the original. He is God's *revelation*, not his *incarnation*. He is the "firstborn of every creature." (Colossians 1:15) "First born" implies a beginning, therefore Christ cannot be the "eternal" Son of God. The Son is "appointed heir"...it is by "inheritance" (Hebrews 1:2) that He has obtained a more excellent name, not by virtue of being a co-equal with His Father.

God said:

> "I am the Lord, Who makes all things, Who stretches out the heavens *all alone*, Who spreads abroad the earth *by Myself...*" (Isaiah 44:24) I *will not* give My glory to another. (Isaiah 48:11)

It is hard to know how God could have made it more clear than that...that He has not and will not share his Deity, even with His own Son.

Believe the Son! Believe God! Believe that Jesus is the Son of God. *Not* God the Son.

> "...for every foolish word which men speak, they will have to answer for it on the day of judgment." (Matthew 12:36)

What could be more foolish than to contradict God and to call His Son a liar? How do you answer to this on the day of judgment?

I know the argument. If the Trinity is false doctrine, why do almost all Christians believe in the Trinity?

Well, why would you believe that something is *right* because a majority believe it? Why do you think that the majority is right, when Jesus, Himself, said:

> "Enter by the narrow gate; for wide is the gate and broad is the way that leads to destruction, and there are many who go in by it. Because narrow is the gate and difficult is the way which leads to life (eternal life) and *there are few who find it.*" (Matthew 7:13-14)

> "Strive to enter in through the narrow door; for I say to you, many will seek to enter in and will not be able." (Luke 13: 24)

> "For many are called but *few are chosen." (Matthew 22:14)*

Again, Paul's letter to Timothy, warned that this would happen. (2 Timothy 4:3-4) It bears repeating:

> "For the time will come when men will not listen to sound doctrine; but will add for themselves extra teachers according to their desires, being lured by enticing words; and they will turn away their ears from the truth, and they will turn to fables."

That's what nearly all churches of today have done...both Catholic and Protestant...very few believe the Truth.

When the shepherds received the message that Christ had been born, "they came hurriedly" to seek Him (Luke 2:16). But "when they spread the word, all who heard were amazed"...but there is no record that any of them rushed off to find Him. (Luke 2:18)

Jesus likened the Kingdom of God to a grain of mustard seed...the tiniest of seeds. (Luke 13:19) It was even questioned whether, when Christ returns, He would really find faith on earth. (Luke 18:8)

Out of the population of millions at the time of the flood, Noah was the only person who was righteous enough to be saved. That's quite a minority, wouldn't you say? His three sons and their wives were saved because of Noah's righteousness...but only Noah qualified.

Millions more populated the cities of Sodom and Gomorrah, but again, God could find only one man, Lot, worth saving. Lot's faith saved his two daughters. Not many out of millions, wouldn't you agree?

> "The harvest is plenty but the workers are few." (Matthew 9:37)

> "The children of the one who is disfavored are more numerous than the children of the one who is favored. " (Galatians 4:27)

Moses sent out 12 scouts to spy on Canaan for 40 days to determine if the land could be taken, as God had said it could. Ten of them came back without faith, saying "no." Only two had faith in God...bringing back the right answer. But *the people went with the majority* and the majority that ruled caused long years of suffering for God's chosen people. (Numbers chapters 13 and 14)

In Luke 17 (verses 12-17) we are told that Jesus met ten Samaritan lepers as he traveled to Jerusalem and sent them to the priest for healing. As they traveled, they were cleansed...healed. One of the ten came back to give praise, falling on his face at Jesus' feet, thanking Him for his healing. Jesus' response to this outpouring of faith was recorded as two questions:
"Were there not ten who were cleansed?" and
"Where are the other nine?"

Being in the majority does not guarantee that Christendom is right.

God will not set up a jury of 12 (or any number) with a *majority* deciding who will enter into His Kingdom. He has clearly set forth the entry rules in the Bible...God's infallible Word...and there is no other way to enter. We should not accept the word of clergy, but must diligently search out the Truth for ourselves.

> "a *few* members...have not defiled their names; and they shall walk with Me in white, for they are worthy." (Revelations 3:4)

Here, Jesus is telling us that there will be only a few who will walk with Him...only a few who will be worthy to be in God's Kingdom. He will not take a vote and accept the beliefs of the majority. God has set down the rules for salvation, and those who ignore them will be left gnashing their teeth.

> "Strive to enter in through the narrow door; for I say to you, many will seek to enter in and will not be able." *(Luke 13:24)*

Truth doesn't change with time. Once God establishes the Truth, it remains firm and immovable. However, humans...and we know that humans have sinful natures...often try to change the Truth into something that is more appealing to them; something that people want to hear or that best suits their own circumstances. That is what happened when humans decided that Jesus should be *God the Son* instead of the *Son of God,* as both Jesus and God told us He was. We can look up every single verse listed in our concordances with the word "God" and we will never find the phrase "God the Son." God is *not* the Son, and the Son is *not* God.

What is wrong with believing that Jesus is God? Nothing...except that it is a lie! Believing a lie will not give you entrance into God's Kingdom.

1 Corinthians 15:28, tells us that Jesus has a lesser status than his Father. When He (Jesus) will have come for His saints...those who have believed in Him in *Truth*... who have had their lives changed because of that belief...those who have been baptized into His church...and who will be kings and princes in the Kingdom...Jesus will, with their help and the help of God's heavenly angels, rule for a thousand years, until all sin and evil is wiped away. Then, God will descend to the sinless earth and Jesus will turn the Kingdom over to His Father. At that time, Jesus will become one of God's subjects, just as all others who are kings and princes in the Kingdom...loving, serving and

worshiping the Father. (1 Corinthians 15:24,28) Jesus, Himself, said His Father is greater than He.

There are more than 2,000 religions in the world and man has invented as many ways to worship as sinful flesh can imagine. By creating their own religion, they have created their own god...*God has not left it to man to decide how to worship Him.* It is not up to humans to decide what is right and what is wrong. God has spelled that out for us in His Scriptures. Through His Son, He warned us of the false prophets that would come, and *THEY ARE HERE!*

Unfortunately, it appears to be human nature to reject anything that challenges our long held, deeply founded beliefs, no matter how incorrect those beliefs or how correct the challenge.

Do not be afraid to turn to the Truth. Yes, people will mock you. Those who call themselves Christians will hate you. But if you believe in any Jesus other than the Jesus that God sent, you cannot expect to receive everlasting life. You cannot expect to avoid the death passed on to us by Adam.

Recommended reading:
The Doctrine of the Trinity (Analytically Examined and Refuted)
By Percy White, Publisher: Stallard & Potter, 2 Jervois St., Torrensville, South Australia 5031
The Doctrine of the Trinity (Christendom's Self Inflicted Wound)
By Anthony Buzzard and Charles Hunting, Publisher: International Scholar Publications, Lanham, New York, Oxford
Bible Basics (A Study Manual – available in 36 languages)
By Duncan Heaster, viewable at http://www.bbie.org
Free copies available at marywarner@attbi.com
http://reslight.addr.com/1john5-7.html
http://www.bible.org/docs/soapbox/1john5-7.htm
http://www.christadelphians.org

THE LIE:
Man Has a Soul That Lives On After Death

"...and if I die before I wake, I pray the Lord my soul to take. Amen."

Children are taught this little prayer from the time they are toddlers and are assured that if they should die in their sleep, Jesus will come and take them to heaven. Meantime, they are assured that Grandma and Grandpa, who have passed away, are already in heaven watching over them and will meet them when they arrive.

"The Bible teaches that whether we are saved or lost, there is conscious and everlasting existence of the soul and personality," says Reverend Billy Graham in his book PEACE AND GOD.

And although anyone who would take the time to study their Bible would know that this is not so, children grow up continuing to believe in an immortal soul that lives on after death.

Early in the life of Christianity, important Bible doctrines were contaminated by the Greeks, even after Greece was conquered by Rome. Greek philosophy had pervaded world learning and the doctrine of the immortal soul, expounded by the reasoning of Plato, was one of the erroneous doctrines introduced to church teachings.

The subject of immortality is clear in Bible teachings. The word appears only five times in the Bible:

(1) 1 Timothy 6:16 – God alone has immortality.
(2) 2 Timothy 1:10 – Jesus Christ brought immortality to light.
(3) Romans 2:7 – We must seek for immortality.
(4) 1 Corinthians 15:53 – Immortality is obtained at the resurrection.
(5) 1 Corinthians 15:54 – Only upon Christ's return can we obtain immortality…can we say "Death is swallowed up in victory."

The word "soul" is used in over eight hundred places in the Bible, and Addendum A, hereto, will show that by referring to several different translations, the word defines itself. It means "life," "each other," "me," "myself," "you," "yourself," "people," "soldiers," and sometimes "heart" or "mind"… and other references to *living*, human creatures, but never to a *part* of a person that survives that person's death.

Like biblical support of any false teaching, a verse can be taken out of context, separated from other defining verses, and forced to "prove" a particular wrong belief. That is what has happened in a few of the over 800 verses which have been pulled out and used to support the doctrine of an "immortal soul."

The passage most frequently used to support such a doctrine is Matthew 10:28.

> "…fear not them which kill the body, but are not able to kill the soul: but rather fear Him which is able to destroy both soul and body…"

Surprisingly, the one verse chosen to prove the belief in the indestructibility of the soul, instead proves that the doctrine is false. *Immortal* means *indestructible*…unable to die. So, while saying that this verse teaches that the soul is immortal…unable to die… it speaks of fearing Him who can kill that which they believe cannot be killed.

What the verse tells us is that man can kill the body, but that is not to be a believer's main concern. This is only a temporary blip on our ultimate existence in God's Kingdom. The One we are to fear is "Him" (God) Who is able to kill the soul...the life that is eternal...able to blot us out of existence forever, and make all of our memories perish. (Deuteronomy 32:39; 1 Samuel 2:6; Ecclesiastes 8:10; 9:4-6; Psalms 31:12; 88:5; Isaiah 26:14.)

> "...both soul and body shall perish and shall be as though they never had been." (Isaiah 10:18)

Here we are told that the soul...the breath of life...will perish as well as the body which will turn to dust.

People who translate the Bible are influenced by their own beliefs, and the translations are then likewise influenced. Not always meaning to lie to their congregations, preachers, pastors, priests, evangelists, etc., often continue the lies that they themselves have been taught. However, many *know* that they are not teaching Truth and will admit that if they told the truth about what the Bible says, they'd be "out of a job."

The children that have been taught to pray for God to take their immortal souls if they die before they wake, ask this of God because they have been told that their souls are separate from their bodies...that their soul lives on after death. In other words, they are influenced in their *prayer* by what they *already believe*...the falsehoods they have been taught.

The idea of a separate soul is one of the ideas picked up from the heathen nations in which the Hebrews lived for so many years...ideas that those heathens had believed for centuries before Christ and which were later hoisted upon the church through the Greek philosophy of Plato during the reign of the Greeks and continued after Rome became the conqueror.

While Psalm 146:3 and 4 tell us that at death a man's thoughts perish, 1 Corinthians 15:52-53 assures those "in Christ" of a life thereafter...*at the time when Christ comes for His church*! Those who are "in Christ" at that time shall "put on immortality." Until that time, death is man's final condition.

> "...there is no work, nor devise, nor knowledge, nor wisdom in the grave where you are going." (Ecclesiastes 9:10)

If man has some part that survives his death, why does Christ come for

His church at all? Robert Roberts, in his book CHRISTENDOM ASTRAY, brings up the same subject.

> "In fact" he says, "it is difficult to see any use for resurrection at all if we accept the popular idea (of the immortal soul) for if man 'goes to his reward' at death, and enjoys all the felicity of heaven of which his nature is capable, it seems incongruous that, after a certain time, he should be compelled to leave the celestial regions, and rejoin his body on earth, when without that body he is supposed to have so much more capability of enjoyment. The resurrection seems out of place in such a system, and accordingly we find that, now-a-days, many are abandoning it, and vainly trying to explain away the New Testament doctrine of physical resurrection"...(pp 58) "...in every instance, popular belief, in reference to the dead, is exactly contrary to the explicit statements of Scripture. It is a belief entirely destitute of foundation." (pp 59) "*There is not a* single promise of heaven at death in the whole Bible, and not a single declaration that man has an immortal soul; and that all the supposed evidence contained in the Bible in favour of these doctrines, is so decidedly ambiguous, as to be open to *disputation as to its meaning.*" (pp 60) "*Death is the* opposite of life; it undoes what birth does."

Why do Christian teachers continue these heathen beliefs in our Sunday Schools when they aren't true? Is the Word of God to be our final authority, or is religious Truth something to be gradually developed by man's speculation on the basis of pagan Greek philosophy? Beginning with the early Roman Church...and followed by the Protestant denominations that grew out of that church...today's Christians, for the most part, have favored the latter.

Another reason there is this belief in an immortal soul is because most are too lazy to learn the Truth. Unfortunately, most people find it more acceptable to sit and listen to their pastor, unquestioningly accepting what he or she tells them, than to go to their Bibles and search out the Truth. This, of course, is what the Bible warns against. It tells us that we should listen with all eagerness, but to "search the Scriptures to see if what they are saying is true." (Acts 17:11) Most don't follow these instructions.

We were warned that false teachers would come, teaching false doctrines and man-made fables. This belief that man has a part that survives his death is certainly one of those "man-made fables" warned against in 2 Timothy 4:3-4.

Another reason the doctrine of the immortal soul is so well accepted is because it is comforting. It doesn't seem to matter that it is a false doctrine. It's an easy belief to accept and it makes us feel good to think that our loved ones who have passed away are still, somehow, hovering around. We don't stop to think of how terrible it would be for that loved one to be looking down and seeing all the horrible things that are going on in the world...or seeing the grief of their loved ones at his or her death.

Anytime you see the word "soul" in the Bible, it will mean "person," "people," "I," "me," "they," "anyone," "everyone," "life," "heart"...or anything that pertains to a living creature...man or beast.

When Romans 13, verse 1 says "let *every soul* be subject to the governing authority," it is telling *every one* to be subject to the government. That must necessarily mean the whole person...a living person.

And in Ephesians 5, verse 19, the King James Version says "speaking to *your souls*" while the Lamsa translation reads "speaking to *one another*."

The various translations of the Bibles, themselves, define "soul." Having studied the more-than-800 times that the word "soul" is used in the Bible, I found that not once has the word been used to refer to some "spiritual" being or part of a being. I invite you to go through your Bible (any and/or all translations) and find some Scripture that says the soul lives on after death. *It isn't there.*

Daniel, who was one of God's greatest prophets, tells us that we shall rest...which, in the Bible, always means to sleep in death...until the end of the days...which in the Bible, always means when the Savior will come and raise us up, giving us incorruptible (immortal) bodies. If Jesus is to change our mortal bodies into immortal bodies, does it make sense that we'll be out of our graves when he comes...off somewhere else...not in the graves from which He is to raise us? We are told the same thing in the New Testament...in 1Corinthians 15:52.

The unmistakable message of the Truth of immortality is in 1 Corinthians 15:20-23:

> "But now Christ is risen from the dead, and has become the firstfruits of those who have fallen asleep (died). For since by man came death, by Man also came the resurrection of the dead. For as in Adam, all die, even so in Christ all shall be made alive. But each in his own order: Christ the firstfruits, afterward those who are Christ's *at His coming.*"

In that same chapter of Corinthians at verses 52 and 53, we are told that not all will die, but that all…even those living *when Christ returns*…will be changed. The dead will be *raised* incorruptible (immortal) and the living will be changed and given the same incorruptible (immortal) bodies that were given to those that had died and were raised first.

When you are thinking about this and when others question you about this belief, you should know that there are many other verses that tell you the same thing. There is Psalms 6, verse 5 that says "In the grave there is *no remembrance.*" Ecclesiastes, chapter 3 verses 19 and 20 explain that when we die, we turn to dust...and that there is no difference in humans and animals after death.

If King David, whom the Bible tells us in Acts 13:22, was "a man after God's own heart" was "dead and buried and *not assigned into the heavens,*" is it likely that any other of the faithful would be assigned to the heavens either?

Daniel was told, too, in Daniel 12:13, to "rest till the end" and that he would "arise" at his "appointed time, *at the end of the days.*"

One more thing to think about. When Jesus died on the cross and was placed in the tomb, is there any record that any part of Him left and went to heaven? Is there any Scripture that shows that He told His disciples that His "soul" flew off to heaven where He saw His Father, God? And wouldn't He surely have told them if such a thing had happened? Jesus remained asleep in the grave until God resurrected Him. If Jesus had to wait to be resurrected, don't you think we will certainly have to wait as well?

Matthew 9:18, 23-25 and Mark 5:35-42 tell us of the time that Jesus raised from the dead the daughter of the synagogue leader. Luke 7:12-15 relates the story of Christ's raising of the widow's son from the dead. We are also told, in John 11:1-44, the details of how Jesus raised Lazarus (Lazar) after he had been dead for 4 days. In addition to those that Christ resurrected, Elisha brought "a dead body to life" (2 Kings 8:5) Paul raised Eutychus (Acts 20:7-12) and Peter raised Tabitha (Acts 9:36-43).

There is not even a hint from any of these people who had died and were raised from the dead, that they had any such experience as a visit to God's heaven...an experience they surely would have related to anyone who would listen. They slept in death until they were raised by God through Jesus, Elisha, Paul, and Peter. But these mortals that were raised from the dead would die again because they were not given immortality. And when they died this time, they will remain dead until Christ returns to judge the earth.

The argument that Jesus told the sinner that died on the cross next to him that he would be with Him in heaven that day is one of the stories taught in Sunday School class to prove that the "soul" goes to heaven at death. Lets read the verse. You'll find it in Luke chapter 23 verse 43.

> "Jesus said to him, truly I say to you, today you will be with me in Paradise."

Now go back and read verse 42. This is where the sinner being crucified with Jesus asks Jesus to remember him.

> "And he said to Jesus, 'remember me, my Lord, when you come in your Kingdom.'"

What an astounding request! It implies that the thief believed that Jesus was Lord; that he knew Jesus would survive the Crucifixion; that Jesus would come into His Kingdom; and that Jesus would be able to remember him. These are the basic New Testament requirements for salvation.

Jesus' reply was:

VERILYISAYTOTHEETODAYTHOUSHALTBEWITHMEINPARADISE.

In the oldest manuscripts, that is how the response appeared. All capitals and no punctuation.

Most translators transcribe the reply to read:
"Verily, I say unto thee, today you shalt be with me in paradise."

But is that correct? Should it not be:
"Verily, I say unto thee today, you shalt be with me in paradise."

Whether the comma is placed before or after "today" tells us what? The thief wanted Jesus to remember him. When? When Jesus sets up His Kingdom. If Jesus told him that he could *tell* him today, the comma would come after "today." Telling him that he could *know* right that minute, that he would be with Him in His Kingdom, he would not have to wait till the Kingdom was established to *know*. But if Jesus is telling him that he will *be* with Him in Paradise today (the comma before "today" as it normally is) we know that cannot be.

Jesus is about to be crucified. In the previous verses, He is telling all who will listen, who He is; why He came; and what it will take for followers to be in His Kingdom. He explains that He does everything that His Father wants Him to do...everything God commands Him to do...even to laying down His life. This thief on the cross next to Jesus heard His words; believed what He said; and wanted to be in the Kingdom.

This is a perfect example explaining the necessity to read more than one verse in deciding what is actually said and meant. The Bible tells us that we must consider all the scriptures together. We need to consider the circumstances at the time things are said; verses before and after the one you are reading; verses recorded at the same time or are written about the same event; who spoke the words; and to whom they were spoken.

Even though most translations place the comma before the word "today," knowing the circumstances of His life and death, all should know that this is not where the comma needed to be. Jesus couldn't have meant that the thief would be *with* Him in paradise *today* because Jesus, Himself, wasn't going to be in paradise *today* and He *knew* that He wasn't. He knew that He was God's Son and He knew exactly what His fate was to be, because He had studied the scriptures. He knew He would be in the tomb for three days, and had spread that word among His disciples. In fact, He was on earth forty days after His resurrection before He went to His Father's house in heaven...and His Kingdom would not be set up until thousands of years later...in fact, has yet to be established.

Not all Bibles do it, but in the Lamsa translation, there is a footnote that says "Ancient texts were not punctuated. The comma could come before or after '*today.*'" If we go back now and read Jesus' answer, putting the comma *after* the word "today," it is clear. "Truly I say to you today, you will be with me in Paradise."

Just by using common sense and knowing a little about the Scriptures, we should know that it *couldn't* mean he would *be* there *today*, the comma can only go in one place...*after* today, in spite of the fact that it appears *before* today in almost all (if not all) translations. Why? Because that supports the false doctrine of the immortal soul which the clergy deceitfully teaches.

A study of the Hebrew custom of speaking in the days of Jesus would also make it clear. He was using a commonly used phrase from the Old Testament. To declare something "this day" (or "today") was a form of solemn statement with full assurance of truth...a well known phrase to underline the seriousness of his words. The thief could be assured that what Jesus promised him, he could rely on to come to pass.

It is plain that this one verse, so often used by Christendom to prove the immortal soul, again disproves the very thing it is set forth to prove.

Ecclesiastes, chapter 12, verse 7 tells us that "when we die, we turn to dust and the spirit returns to God." This verse is often misread to say "*our* spirit returns to God," but the spirit of which it speaks is *the* spirit, not *our* spirit...that which leaves is the same spirit that gave life to Adam. When God withdraws that spirit (or breath) nothing is to be left but that which existed before God gave it...dust.

"If God should gather to Himself *His* spirit all flesh would perish together, and man would return to dust."

Again, *God's* spirit, not ours. (Job 34:14-15)

There is one place in the Bible that tells us specifically that there is no consciousness of any kind after death. Job 14:21, tells us that after we are dead, our loved ones may receive many honors and we don't know anything about it...or they can be dishonored, and we don't know that either. It is pretty clear that we won't know anything after death until Jesus comes again.

Man is mortal. There is no part of him that is immortal, therefore, no part of him lives on after his death. Ecclesiastes 9:5-6 makes this an unquestionable truth.

> "For the living know that they shall die; but the dead know nothing..."

> "God...has made one thing opposite to another, to the end that *man should know nothing after he is gone*." *(Ecclesiastes 7:14)*

We are told in Job 14, verses 12 and 21, that when man dies he does not rise again...that he does not awake nor is he roused out of this sleep of death.

> "...they shall not awake, nor be raised out of their sleep... if his sons multiply, he does not know it; if they decrease, he perceives it not..."

Job also spells out clearly, that a destiny of decay awaits human beings at death.

> "Man decays, like a rotten thing; like a garment that is moth-eaten." (13:28) "Man dies and fades away; yea, man perishes and *he is no more." (Job:14:10)*

The real problem is that most do not know what the word "soul" means. It is thought of (and from the pulpit is taught to be) some spiritual part of a person that lives on after death. But in Hebrews 9:27 we are told that *"man is destined to die once and after that to face Judgment..."* and we know that all are to be judged at the same time...not one at a time as we die.

But in spite of what churches teach, at death humans perish! They pass away completely. No part of them lives on, and most certainly they are not in heaven "watching over those they loved," as we have been led to believe.

The doctrine of the immortal soul lived among pagans for thousands of years before it was advanced through Greece, to Rome, and into Christianity, and it is clear from the attempt by terrorists to be delivered to 72 virgins in some far off paradise, that it is a belief that still exists by many. Yet, the most surprising thing of my research was to find that until the 1800s, the *doctrine of the immortal soul* was admitted, by theologians, to have been based on Greek philosophy. In fact, those who introduced the idea were proud to have developed "many improvements" upon what they consider the hazy concepts voiced by the *"Holy men of God."* These supporters of the "immortal soul" doctrine were frank to admit that the concept *did not come from the Bible.*

Many are fascinated by "Psychics" who profess to be able to talk to the dead and receive messages for them from dead loved ones. But God tells us that these people who "inquire of the dead concerning the living" are not from God. (Isaiah 8:19).

However, in spite of what God says, leaders of Christendom have wrested the Scriptures for verses to "prove" such a doctrine.

> "Beware lest any man mislead you through *philosophy* and vain deceit, after the teachings of men, after the principle of the world..." (Colossians 2:8)

Since we all know that to "perish" is to be destroyed completely, we should understand that when man dies, all of him dies.

In the very first book of the Bible...Genesis 2:7...we are told what a soul is. It is a combination of dust and the breath of God. It takes both to be a soul. If God takes away His breath, all that is left is dust.

Genesis 2:7 reads:

> "And the Lord God formed man of the dust of the ground, and

breathed into his nostrils the breath of life; and man became a living soul."

Man *became* a living soul. That's exactly what a soul is. A living being. A whole, living being. When God made man out of the dust, all He had was the form of a man...like a statue. Not until He breathed life into this statue did it become a living person...a living soul. The King James translation of the Bible actually says "a living soul," but in recent years, the use of "living being" appears to be more understandable, because that's exactly what 'soul' means: a living breathing creature.

Before man was made a "living soul," God made animals as the first "living souls." Anything that breathes through it's nostrils is a "soul," but *none is immortal.* The words "immortal soul" do not appear in the Bible, and the idea that it conveys is not there either. Throughout the Bible, the word soul infers "life"...to both man and beast. (Genesis 1:24; 1:26; and 1:30)

Since most of the Bible dictionaries and commentaries are written by Trinitarians influenced by their own beliefs, it is sometimes better to go to a secular source that is devoted solely to the defining of words in order to get a true definition.

Webster's Dictionary:
"The Christian conception of the soul derives from the Greek, especially as modified by the mystery cults..."

Funk and Wagnall Dictionary:
"Among the ancient Hebrews 'soul' was the equivalent of the principle of life as embodied in living creatures, and this meaning is continued throughout the Bible..."

Hassting's Bible Dictionary:
"soul is throughout a great part of the Bible simply the equivalent of 'life' embodied in living creatures."

The International Standard Bible Encyclopedia:
"Soul has various shades of meaning in the Old Testament, which may be summarized as follows: living being, life, self, person, desire,

appetite, emotion and passion."

Strong's Concordance:
"Soul: A breathing creature, an animal; or, abstractly, vitality."

The Encyclopedia Britannica:
"Among Old Testament Israelites and New Testament Christians, the human being was considered to be an organismic unit so that the Hebrew word 'nefesh' and the Greek word 'soul' referred to the functioning unit of an individual *rather than some part of him...In other words, the soul was the living mortal person and not a homesick visitor from the eternal region, and there was nothing about the living mortal person, in part or as a whole, which was expected to survive the death of the functioning organism."* (Emphasis provided)

In applying "soul" to both man and animal, the scriptures seem to be taking special care to protect us from this false concept of an immortal soul. We need to avoid these philosophical teachings against which the Apostle Paul so vehemently warned.

The noted lexicographer, Parkhurst, himself a believer in the doctrine of the immortal soul, admits that he could find no passage in the Bible that "soul" has such a meaning.

We do not have to go to the encyclopedia, however, to learn the definition of the word "soul." The Bible, itself, defines it for us.

In order to make it easier, I obtained seven different translations of the Bible, and I have gone through each. Where the word "soul" appears in one translation, I have made a note of that verse and have then checked each of the other translations to see if any of them used a different word.

For example:
"...that *soul* shall be cut off from his people..."
This is a quotation from the King James Version

"...that *person* shall be cut off from his people..."

As it appears in the New King James, Lamsa and Revised versions.

"...any...*male*...shall be cut off from his people..."
From the NIV translation.

"...*anyone*...shall be cut off from his people..."
When used in the Living Bible.

Another verse used by most who call themselves Christians, to prove their belief in an immortal soul, is 2 Corinthians 5:6,8.

> "As long as we are at home in the body, we are absent from our Lord...This is why we are confident and anxious to be absent from the body and to be present with our Lord."

Clergy raise their arms and their voices, screaming "*Absent from the body, present with the Lord*"...meaning, *they say*, that the moment you die you are instantly with God.

Paul, whose life was devoted to teaching the Gospel of the Kingdom of God and Jesus Christ, and in encouraging others to do the same, would never be suggesting that he (or they) with so much to accomplish for God, should be anxious to die (for any reason).

We know now, having studied the passages presented earlier, that both the Old Testament and the New, tell us that we do not appear in heaven at the moment of death. (There is rarely a reference made to where the evil go at the instant of death.) Although most of Christendom teaches (in support of it's doctrine of the immortal soul) that there is instant transfer from the death bed to heaven, no such belief is supported by Scripture. Knowing this to be the case, then what is the meaning of 2 Corinthians 5:6 and 8?

This passage contains just one of the wordings of the many messages that Paul preached on the same subject during his ministry.

Paul, in this letter to the Corinthians, is teaching the same lesson of change that he has been expounding since his conversion. No one could be more qualified to teach such a lesson than Paul. He persecuted the believers to the point of capturing and killing them...until Jesus appeared to him and made a believer of him. Paul knew more about changing from sin to righteousness than even those chosen by Jesus to be His apostles...and this was a message on which Paul dwelt throughout his teaching years.

In his letter to the Romans, he uses different words *but the message is the same.* He explains that when believers are baptized into Jesus Christ, the sinful body is *destroyed* and such baptized believer should no longer serve sin; i.e., should be "absent from the body"...away from his sinful, natural, worldly self. He explains that we must consider ourselves "dead *to* sin but alive *from* sin through Jesus Christ"; in other words, having put off sin, we are "present with the Lord." (Romans 6:13)

> "...you were buried with Him (Christ) in baptism in which you were also raised with Him." (Colossians 2:12)

> "Do not present yourselves as instruments of unrighteousnessto sin, but present yourselves to God as being *alive from the dead*, and your bodies as instruments of righteousness." (Romans 6:13)

> "...if Christ is in you, the *body is dead* because of sin, but the *spirit is life* because of righteousness." (Romans 8:10)

> "Therefore, if anyone is in Christ, he is a new creation; old things have passed away; behold, all things have become new." (2 Corinthians 5:17)

"Absent from the body" simply means the putting aside of our sinful proclivities; and to be "present with the Lord" describes the new life of those who have been "born again" through the acceptance of, and baptism into, Jesus Christ. This is a popular teaching of Paul throughout his ministry...an urging to the followers of Christ to lay aside their sinful lives and become "born again" in Jesus Christ.

The same message was clearly set forth in 1 Peter 2:24, when he said that Jesus "bore our sins in His own body on the tree, that we having *died to sin*, might *live to righteousness."*

If Paul had realized that church clergy were going to teach *only* from 2 Corinthians 5:6-8, he might have made the verses more easily understandable by inserting parenthetical explanations, such as:

> "As long as we are at home (contented and satisfied) in the body (in our sinful nature) we are absent from our Lord (we are not spiritual in our worship)…This is why we are confident and anxious to be absent from the body (anxious to overcome our natural, sinful selves) and to be present with our Lord (to be more spiritual in our lives)."

A study of Paul's total teachings give clarity to 2 Corinthians 5:6-8. In Romans 6:11, he covers the same subject, using slightly different wording.

> "…you also must consider yourself as being *dead to sin,* but *alive to God* through Jesus Christ our Lord."

The disciples often spoke of those who were believers as not being "of the world." (1 John 4:4-6) Those "in Christ" are instructed not to be "of the world." In all instances, they are being told to keep themselves spiritually minded and not to dwell on the things of the world.

There is nothing that survives the death of a human being (or an animal, for that matter)…no "soul" that flies off to heaven at death.

The attached Addendum A will provide you with hundreds of the verses defining "soul" as a living, breathing being or beings…not some part of a person. Part of us doesn't die and leave another part alive.

There are no uses of the word 'soul', either in the Old Testament or the New, that prove…or even support…the notion of an immortal soul. There are a few, however (which we have mentioned) that can be forced to fit the immortal soul idea *only* if we are willing to ignore all the rest of the Scriptures.

In the Old Testament, alone, the word "nephesh" (translated in English to "soul") has several meanings. In the King James Version, 119 times as "life"; 25 times as "person"; 16 times as "heart"; and 15 times as "mind"…and *never is it spoken of as immortal.*

God created Adam; gave him a free will; placed him in the Garden of Eden where there were two trees...one, the Tree of Life; one, the Tree of Knowledge of Good and Evil, warning him that death would be the result of eating from the Tree of Knowledge; and God left Adam to make his own decision. He chose to eat of the tree that would result in mortality. Once he had made that decision, God locked him out of the Garden and put guards at the gates so that he could no longer have access to the Tree of Life...no longer could choose immortality. (Genesis 3)

We are the descendants of Adam and have inherited the same fate that he chose...mortality. Immortal life is available only through God's begotten Son, to be bestowed by Him *upon His return for His church.* (1 Corinthians 15:52-53)

Man's only hope is to learn, *while we are alive,* what the *Truth* is, to live in it, and to teach it to others so that when Christ returns we will be worthy to receive the immortal life that is promised.

Just because you believe the teachings of your spiritual leader, does not assure you a place in God's Kingdom. Your Bible is the place that will tell you whether your clergyman or clergywoman is teaching you the Truth.

> "...the ungodly shall *perish.*" (Psalms 1:6)
> "...man shall *know nothing* after he is dead." (Ecclesiastes 7:14)

Jesus "brought life and immortality to life *through the Gospel.*" (2 Timothy 1:10) It was not until after the Gospel...after Jesus Christ...that *immortality* became a possibility for man. And Jesus did not tell us that when He died, a part of Him flew off to be with God. It was 40 days later that He ascended to meet His Father.

To those who study the Scriptures, it becomes evident that the teachings of today's churches (that man has always had an immortal part) *is false.*

Either we accept the teachings of the Bible, or we do not. If we do not, then we should not call ourselves Christians, for the very foundation of Christianity is *supposed* to be the Bible.

THE LIE:
Heaven Will Be The Believer's Eternal Home

We now know that no part of us will fly off to heaven *upon death.* The question, then, is will believers *ever* go to heaven? To hear the teachings of Christendom's clergy, you would have to answer "yes." To search out the answer in the Bible, it's not so definite. Heaven is certainly not to be the location of God's eternal Kingdom.

Nearly all of Christendom teaches that if we are "saved" we will spend eternity in heaven. But nowhere in the Bible are we told that we will *ever* go to heaven, no matter how "saved" we might be.

My granddaughter says that "Jesus will take us to the Kingdom He sets up in heaven…just like the criminal that died on the cross next to His."

However, the Scriptures don't tell us that the Kingdom Jesus sets up will be in heaven.

Take a look at Luke 11:2.

> "And He said to them, when you pray say: Our Father who art in heaven, hallowed be Your name. *Your kingdom come*. Your will be done *on earth* as it is in heaven."

This verse describes to us where God's Kingdom *is*…not where it will be when believers reign with Christ. In fact, Jesus is telling us to pray for God's heavenly kingdom to *come*...and for His will to be done *on earth,* just as it is in heaven.

Do you think Jesus would tell us to pray for something that would never be?

Yes, Preachers say (as does the Bible) that our rewards are being stored up in heaven, so they insist that we have to go there to get them. Why? We are told in Revelations 22:12 that Jesus will bring our reward with Him when He comes to judge the works of those who are in Christ.

"Jesus is going to rule in God's Kingdom for a thousand years," they teach, and since Jesus is in heaven, then that's where believers will be going. That's not what the Bible tells us.

Our pastors also tell us that when Jesus ascended into heaven He told His followers that He was going to prepare a place for them, so surely they would have to *go to heaven,* to that place that He is preparing. Not necessarily. The *preparations* are being made in heaven, but we know, if we study our Bibles at all, that the preparations are for a Kingdom on earth...more specifically, in Jerusalem.

Jesus wrote us a letter, known as the Revelation, which He dictated to John in a dream. In it, He warned the churches that they were not teaching the Truth. Yes, false teachings were cropping up in the churches even then. But in this letter, Jesus also described where His Kingdom will be. He showed John, in this dream, the new Jerusalem (the Kingdom that had been *prepared* in heaven) *coming down* from heaven. And isn't that the very thing that Jesus told us to pray for when he taught us to pray "thy Kingdom come..."?

In the first chapter of Acts, in the 9th verse, we're told how Jesus went up into heaven, and then, in verse 11, that *He will come down again in the same way He left.* When He makes His appearance, those who have died in Christ will be raised up first. Those believers who are still living when He comes will be next, and all those, living and raised from the dead, *that are in Christ* will be made immortal and will be with Him forever after. That is told in no uncertain terms in First Thessalonians, chapter 4, verse 16. But even with all the Believers assembled with Him, nothing says that, even then, they would be going to God's heaven. Only that they would *meet with Him in the air* and would then *be with Him* forever...no matter where He was to be.

But what is the requirement to be "in Christ"? The requirement is that you *know who Jesus is*; that you believe that He is God's Son; that you understand that He died as a sacrifice for mankind, just as we will die; that He rose again from the dead so that we, too, may some day rise again and have eternal life in God's Kingdom. Once you know these Truths...understand and truly believe them...Jesus tells you to "be baptized" in His name. (Acts 10:48)

If you truly believe this, it will change your life...which means you are "born again" to a new life (John 3:3; Romans 8:10)...you will then, upon baptism, be *"in Christ"* (Romans 6:3; 12:5) ...a son or daughter of God (Romans 8:14)...an adopted brother or sister to Jesus...a seed (a descendent) of Abraham...a Jew in God's eyes. God promised the Kingdom to Abraham's descendants, and we can become children of Abraham by accepting Jesus as our Savior.

The doctrine of Christ's reign upon earth...though it is spelled out clearly in the Bible...has, by degrees, become a doubtful and useless opinion, rejected and called heresy and fanaticism in a well organized church with political aspirations. As a result, the Roman Catholic Church proclaimed itself the Kingdom of God! Such a determination caused the Church to worry more about the present than about the future of Christ's rule.

Believing themselves to be living in holiness, many men and women went into monasteries, separating themselves from family life or any normal, well balanced association with others. The Bible does not advocate such isolation and social ostracism. Ephesians 4:13-16 points out the necessity and importance of human relationships between all of Christ's followers.

But out of this type of life...this separation from others...the church began to elevate some of its members as "holy men" and invested them with sainthood, considering them as "lesser gods."

The many pagans, who were already accustomed to worshiping a variety of male and female deities, were easily convinced that they should change their love and affection, bestowing it on these new gods...these so-called saints.

Gibbon (in his "Decline and Fall," vol. 4, pp 6-8) pointed out:

> "Ambition soon discovered the secret road which led to the possession of wealth and honors…The monasteries were filled by a crowd of obscure and abject plebeians who gained in the cloister much more than they had sacrificed in the world."

1 Peter 5:2 instructs Believers to preach willingly and with a ready mind, *but not for money.* That is an instruction rarely heeded. Large denominations pay their pastors many hundreds of thousands of dollars a year to "lead the flock."

Over the years, countless millions of Christians have been destined to perish because the church would tolerate no questioning of its authority. The Roman Church, by virtue of the power of the priesthood and papacy, assumed monumental proportions; dominating political rulers; interfering in international affairs; and invading every aspect of private life by devising the educational system that taught its member that the Pope is infallible…that he speaks for God.

However, none of this is a surprise to Bible scholars, who know that Paul warned of it.

> "For I know this," he said, "that after my departing shall grievous wolves enter in among you, not sparing the flock. Also, *of your own selves* shall men arise, speaking perverse things, to draw away disciples after them." (Acts 20:29-30)

Revelation 5, verse 10, assures us that Jesus will reign on His throne *on the earth* and that those in Christ shall reign with Him *on earth.* Again, He's telling us that the Kingdom will be on earth.

There are no contradictions in the Bible. When we find two verses that *seem* to tell us different things, we need to look at them carefully and see which one is told in clear language that can only mean one thing. If we read John 14:2 quickly, we assume Jesus was preparing a place for us to *go to* in heaven. But that contradicts the Scripture that says, clearly, "we will reign on *earth."*

Knowing that, we need to go back to John and see if there is any way that this could mean something we hadn't seen before. The clear language of Revelation is telling us that Jesus' Kingdom will be on earth. Then we can see that John, is not giving us the location of the eternal Kingdom, but is telling us where the *preparations* for that Kingdom are being made. Having examined both Scriptures, we see that there is no contradiction. This is our way of reconciling the two. The message is clear.

The thief on the cross is another example. (Luke 23:43) By searching other Scriptures, we found that the common belief couldn't possibly be correct. Jesus wasn't *in* Paradise that day...He wasn't *going to be in Paradise* that day, and He knew that it would be at least 3 days before He would go into heaven to be with His Father. So by learning that, we know that Jesus certainly wasn't telling the thief that he'd be with Him some place that He wasn't going to be. We need to be very careful to make certain that we don't just grab one Scripture and rely on it without checking it against others.

It bears repeating that in the early days, when the Bible was being translated, all the letters of the words were in capitals, no spaces and no punctuation.

ITELLYOUTODAYYOUWILLBEWITHMEINPARADISE is the way the ancient Scripture appeared.

The comma in the message that Jesus gave to the thief was inserted, by the translators, in the wrong place. Instead of reading "I tell you, today you will be with me in Paradise..." (something that couldn't be true) the comma should have been *after* "today," reading: "I *tell you today*, you will be with me in paradise."

The Lamsa translation has a footnote that reads: "Ancient texts were not punctuated. The comma could come before or after 'today.'"

Jesus made no promise that the thief would be with Him in paradise that day (a place that Jesus wasn't even, Himself, going to be). He was telling the thief that he wouldn't have to wait till He, Jesus, was in the Kingdom to *know*...Jesus was *telling him today* that he would be there when the Kingdom was established.

Unfortunately, many people fail to truly examine the Scriptures to learn their True meaning. They either accept what is told them from the pulpit or they latch onto a meaning they like and accept it as gospel. That's why so much of God's message is missed...and why many who believe they are saved will end up in eternal separation from God...eternal death.

We never know it all. We never understand every word of the Bible. We can study it all of our lives and always find something we'd failed to see before. The main thing to remember is that we need to study it *continually.*

After Jesus has reigned on earth for a thousand years with His princes, kings and saints...ruling over and converting new disciples, and ridding the world of all sin, *God* will come to take over.

We tend to forget, I believe, that when Christ comes to set up God's Kingdom, there will be ordinary, mortal people still on the earth...those who have not accepted the True Jesus nor obeyed His commandments...even some who have never heard of Jesus. It is these mortals to whom those who have been saved will minister. That is the job of those saints who will have been raised and immortalized.

Since God cannot abide in the presence of sin, by the time Jesus completes His thousand year reign over the Kingdom, there will be no more crime; no more harshness; no more crippling diseases or illness; no more rage or unhappiness; no more terrorism; just love and worship and music. Then God can come and take over, and once He does, Jesus will become one of God's subjects, just as those who are "in Christ" will be his subjects. (1 Corinthians 15:28)

We cannot be dogmatic about whether or not Believers *ever* go to heaven. Most of Christendom believes they do...at death. Other denominations with a clearer understanding of the Scriptures, believe they do not. There is no Scripture that says *definitively* that the righteous go to heaven...but the references to the occasion referred to as "the Rapture"...the time when

Jesus comes "for His church"...for "His bride"... together with a study of the way the Hebrew marriages occurred, could certainly support such a belief.

Jesus said that He would "come again" and receive Believers to Himself. The Scriptures tell us that He will come "in the clouds," as a thief in the night, and that those *asleep in Christ (dead)* will rise first, followed by those that are *in Christ but are still alive. They will all* join Him in the air and will *"ever be with the Lord."* (1 Thessalonians 4:16-17).

The question, then, is *where* will they be with the Lord? It doesn't say they will be in heaven; it doesn't say they will be on earth; and some believe that they won't even stay "in the clouds."

Many believe that "in the clouds" is a biblical expression, meaning "in a crowd" or "in a multitude" or as "an elevation of status," and these are certainly manners of speaking often used in the Bible. But in this particular instance, it does not appear to be correct.

When Jesus was ascending into heaven to be with His Father after His resurrection, He was with disciples and "a cloud received Him out of their sight." This was no "crowd" or "multitude" or "elevation of status," but billowing clouds as we know them. Two men stood by them dressed in white who said to the men of Galilee, "Why do you stand gazing up into heaven? This same Jesus, who was taken up from you into the heavens, *will so come in like manner as you saw Him go into heaven."* (Acts 1:9-11)

This tells us that when Jesus returns for His church, He will come in the clouds of heaven and Believers will join Him there and "will ever be with the Lord."

To believe in Jesus Christ is to have a conviction that He is who the Bible says He is and that He will do what He promises...and He promises that "he who believes in Him who sent Me has everlasting life and shall not come into judgment, but has passed from death into life." (John 5:24)

When Jesus returns for His church, those who have accepted Christ as their Savior, have obeyed Him and have not fallen away, will be given what they were promised...EVERLASTING LIFE WITHOUT FURTHER

JUDGMENT FOR SIN. (John 5:24) However, every believer must stand before the judgment seat of Christ for an evaluation (judgment) of their earthly deeds in the service of the Lord and the handing out, or withholding, of rewards based thereon. (2 Corinthians 5:10)

It is here that we are left to wonder where this judgment will take place.

Some believe that the church will be taken off to some far away, earthly wilderness for the judgment. But Isaiah 13 tells of the day of the Lord's wrath; and fierce anger that will destroy sinners; of the events of the Great Tribulation; of God's punishment of the world for its evil and of the wicked for their iniquity; and that mankind, for the most part, will be destroyed. During this period, 2/3 of all the people *on earth* are massacred. The remaining 1/3 do not repent. It is comforting to know that "God has *not* appointed His Believers to such wrath." (1 Thessalonians 5:9) With such a promise, can we possibly believe that, after the snatching away of the church, there could be Believers still on earth where all the promised devastation will be taking place?

Others believe that both Christ and those that are "in Christ" will remain "in the air" until He returns to earth to set up the Kingdom. Who are we to say whether this is likely?

Many believe that the faithful will be taken to heaven for this judgment (this assignment of duties in the Kingdom), where they may even meet with God prior to the establishment of His earthly Kingdom. A study of Hebrew customs makes this third choice seem, if not the most likely, certainly possible.

> "In my Father's house are many mansions; if it were not so I would have told you. I go to prepare a place for you. And if I go and prepare a place for you, I will come again and receive you to Myself, and where I am, there you may be also." (John 14:2-3)

This does not tell us that we will go to heaven...to His Father's house...to the place being prepared; only that He will come again for us and that we will be with Him. But neither does it tell us that we will *not* go to heaven. And frankly, I don't believe that the way we feel about this particular thing has anything to do with our salvation. However, lets look at Hebrew customs.

A father in a Hebrew family would choose a bride for his son, sometimes many years before any marriage was to take place. When the time was right, the Son would go and get his bride and take her to his father's house for the marriage feast.

This is exactly the way the Bible describes Christ's Appearance, referred to by many as the Rapture. God, His Father, will have chosen those that are to be saved...those who are to be "in Christ"...in His church. He has chosen His Son's bride.(Acts 15:14; Romans 8:28-29; 2 Thessalonians 2:13; 1 Peter 2:4, 9; Revelation 17:14) Then after His death, Jesus, the Son, went to His Father's house to prepare a place for His "bride." (John 14:2-3) When the time is right, Christ will come for His "bride"...His "church"...and will take her to His Father's house, as was the Hebrew custom. Since God's house is in heaven, could He not take His church there?

Whether Christ takes His church to heaven *at this point in time* is, I believe, immaterial. However, to believe...and to preach...that *God's eternal Kingdom* is to be in heaven, is a false doctrine that will keep those who believe it from entering that Kingdom. We have been instructed to preach "the Kingdom of God." (Luke 9:60) Because it is God's eternal Kingdom that we are to preach, it is necessary that we know what and where it will be...and it will be in Jerusalem!

Now is the time to defy the "Universal Church." Not just the Roman Catholic church, but all denominations that have been influenced by her apostasy.

> "Come out of her, that ye be not partakers of her sins, and that ye receive not of her plagues." (2 Corinthians 6:17- 18; Matthew 6:22-23)

Only the Bible can guide Christians into the Kingdom of God, and the Bible assures us that once we embrace its messages, we will dwell with Christ on earth...in Jerusalem...and that after serving with Him for a thousand years, His Father...*our* Father...will come down to take over this then perfect world.

THE LIE:
Christ Existed Before His Birth (Is Eternal)

"...and God said, let us make man in our image, after our likeness." (Genesis 1:26)

The use of the plurals "us" and "our" assures those who believe in Jesus' pre-existence, that their belief is true. These (God, Jesus and perhaps the Holy Spirit) are the "us" and "our" after which the man Adam was patterned, they say. But this proves their belief *only* if you fail to study the Scriptures to see that such a pre-existence would be impossible.

The persons after whom Adam was fashioned were, doubtless, God and the angels which dwelt, and dwell, in heaven with Him and have, throughout the Scriptures, been agents of God in His work. In both the Old and New Testaments, angels were mistaken for men, and therefore this first earthly man must surely have been patterned after these angels.

In Genesis 18, when three messengers of God...angels...came to Abraham, they came as men. When the angels came to Lot in Genesis 19, he mistook them for men. And the Apostles and Disciples were admonished not to forget to entertain strangers (humans) for they might be entertaining "angels unaware." (Hebrews 13:2)

Likewise, we who are Believers and are to be resurrected in the last days, will be like angels. (Luke 20:36) We do not know where the angels that reside with God in heaven came from. What we do know is that they are God's messengers. The word "angel" *means* messenger. My own suspicion is that the heavenly angels are the saints of a former creation...an earlier universe...and are those who received their salvation in whatever way God set up for them in that time and place. We do not know. We only know that they too, are children of God, and that we who are saved will be like them upon our resurrection...and therefore will join them in assisting Jesus in ruling the Kingdom when He returns. (Luke 20:36)

Nearly all of Christendom believes...*because they are told*...that Jesus existed with God before His birth. If Jesus had been with God from before the beginning, would there not have been some indication of this in God's Holy Scriptures? Some explicit statement, not inferred from another?

"Oh, but there is!" a Trinitarian will tell you. Revelation 22:13 says that Jesus is the "Alpha and Omega, the Beginning and the End, the First and the Last."

This, they insist, shows that Jesus was with God from the beginning and was the first creation of God. On the contrary, this verse proves that Jesus is *NOT* God. God had no beginning, but was and is eternal.

If we study the Scriptures more thoroughly, however, we know that Revelation 22:13 does not speak of the same "beginning" as the Genesis "beginning" which describes God's creation of the universe. In the Revelation verse, in which Jesus Himself was speaking of being the "beginning," He is speaking of the beginning of the church...the "creation of new men and women." In the New Testament, the words "create" or "creation" are often used to mean "regeneration."

For example:

> In Ephesians 2:10, we are told that the disciples are "created" in Christ, as His workmanship, and that such creation was ordained by God.
>
> In Ephesians 4:24, that the disciples "put on the new man which was "created" according to God...";

Galatians 6:15, describing how, if we are "in Christ," we become a "new creation"; and in

2 Corinthians 5:17, reiterates that if we are "in Christ" we are "new creations."

Jesus is the *beginning* of this *new creation*...the first to live, die and receive life eternal. (Revelation 1:18; 2:8) He is the "Alpha and Omega; the First and the Last" of this new creation...the creation which commenced with Christ's death and resurrection, the "firstborn from the dead." (Colossians 1:18)

From the seventh chapter of the second book of Samuel, we learn that instead of letting David build a house for God, the Lord would build a house for David...but not during David's lifetime. It would be built by a *descendant* of David's...his son Solomon. After making this disclosure of things to come, God added a remarkable statement, set forth in 2 Samuel 7:14:

"I will be His Father and He shall be My Son."

This was a type; a shadow; a pointing forward to the time when God would say almost the exact words about Jesus *before His birth.* As set forth in Hebrews 1:5, His words were:

"I will be to Him a Father and He shall be to Me a Son."

Note that the statement in Samuel was made prior to the birth of Solomon and hundreds of years prior to the birth of Jesus; and the statement recorded in Hebrews was made prior to the birth of Jesus.

If those who insist that this statement about Jesus proves that he pre-existed with God before His birth, shouldn't they also insist that the same statement must have been proof that Solomon was also in heaven with God before *he* was born? Yet we never hear such an argument.

If Jesus had already been in existence with God in heaven, instead of "I *will be* His Father and He *shall be* My Son," God would have said, "I *am* His Father and He *is* My Son."

These were prophesies of things that were to happen in the future...and the relationship between God and Jesus was also to be a *future* relationship as Father and Son.

Calvary Chapel's Chuck Smith, in teaching that Jesus lived with God before His birth, uses John 1:1-3, saying that the word "Word" means Logos (which it does) and that Logos is another name for Jesus (which it isn't).

What I found when I searched out and studied the word "Logos" was certainly not supportive of Pastor Smith's teachings...but then, of course, I was not looking into books written by presidents of Trinitarian universities and schools.

In encyclopedias, I found that the word "Logos" which is, in fact, "Word," as "signifying a structure and activity inherent in the cosmos, similar to human reason"; "the term to designate the ordering pattern that is half hidden, half recognizable in the flux of the world"; "the ceaseless movement of nature"; "the ordering principal of the universe, a germinal power"; "the wisdom of God"; "the rational structure and timeless truth"; "the reason of God"; "an imminent law of nature"; "the word of God"; "to say"; "governs all things"; "has the function of correcting deviations from the eternal law that rules things"; "Like a law of nature, objective in the world, it gives order and regularity to the movement of things and makes the system rational"; "the principle which sets all nature under the rule of thought, and directs it towards a rational end, or the divine spirit itself"; "the principle of the active reason working in dead matter"; "a reason in the world gifted with intelligence, and analogous to the reason in man"; "the divine dynamic, the energy and self-revelation of God"; "God's creative, illuminative and redemptive activity"; and "the expression of God's will and power, the outgoing of the divine energy, life and light." In one word, God's "Word," or "logos" might be called God's "Will and Plan."

At least these were the meanings of "Logos" before the Trinitarians needed scripture to support a false theory of an eternal Jesus, and defined and personified "Logos" as "Jesus"...*centuries after His death.*

The gospel according to John is a highly philosophical work containing many speeches of the Lord Jesus which require careful analysis and study. Such an approach is rendered more difficult by the problems which arise when one has to express, in English, something which originally was taught in Greek. This difficulty is apparent in the very first verse of this Book because of that one word which John uses. This is the Greek word "Logos" which is translated as "Word" and is (since the advent of the Trinity doctrine) taught to be another name, or title, for Jesus.

In the Bible, "logos" is translated 8 times as "account"; 3 times as "communication"; 4 times as "matter"; 50 times as "saying"; 8 times as "speech"; 4 times as "thing"; 208 times as "word"...meaning preaching; 7 times as "word" with a capital "W"; and twice as "reason."

It is most reasonable to translate "logos" as "the Plan and Purpose of God as it was manifested by the Lord Jesus Christ," for the following reasons:

The Greek word "logos" is used as a suffix in several English words such as:

"ecoLOGY" - the concept of the balance of nature;

"archaeoLOGY"- the concept of very old;

"geoLOGY" - the concept of the earth.

All these come from the Greek word "logos" translated in John 1:1 as "Word."

The LOGICal conclusion is that John is referring to the great Divine Concept of Creation and Self-manifestation which God had before *anything* was created.

Jesus was a pre-existent *plan* in the mind of God...not a pre-existent *person*.

God knew from before the beginning, that man, as He would create him, would not be able to live by the laws that He would set down; that man would sin; and that He would have to send His Son to heal the world. And Jesus was not the first one, nor the first time, God had said He had known of births before they occurred and had planned the purpose of such a birth. God told Jeremiah that "before I formed you in the belly, ***I knew you***, and before you came out of the womb, *I sanctified you and ordained you* a priest to the nations." (Jeremiah 1:5) Surely no one teaches that Jeremiah existed with God before *he* was born?

As a simple anaLOGY, imagine that we have designed in our minds a house that we want to build one day. We think a lot about it, but nothing happens until we take action towards obtaining the materials. Once we do that, the plans that we had in our minds long ago become tangible. We did not have even the paper plans, nor the walls, floors, doors, windows, etc., with us in the beginning. All we had were the mental plans.

Likewise, God had a Plan, the LOGOS, with Him before the beginning. Just as one cannot be separated from one's thought, so in that sense, the LOGOS was God because it was His *Plan* of the manifestation of Himself...(Romans 16:26) "...all the earth shall be filled with the glory of the LORD." (Numbers 14:21)

But before this could happen, there had to be an earth; there had to be the sun, moon and stars; there had to be all the creatures that make up nature, both animate and inanimate; and there had to be people...and finally, there had to be a Savior. *The Plan* for all these were with God before time began.

As Paul said in Hebrews 1:1-2, that God was *revealed* to man in various ways. These methods of communication from God to man were:

by the Universe (which He created);

by promises (which God made to His faithful);

by visitations from angels (which were God's messengers);

by visions and dreams (sent to His prophets and faithful);

by the *spoken word* (of those prophets);

by the *written* words (of those whom God chose to write His Scriptures);

and eventually, He was revealed through a Life (that of His Son, Jesus Christ). Jesus was the greatest of all these ways that God chose to convey his "Logos"...His Plan...Himself... to mankind.

Hebrews makes it clear that God did not speak to mankind through His

Son in the Old Testament, but only after His birth as a human...as a flesh and blood person. This is a compelling argument that there was no Father-Son relationship before Jesus' birth...that Jesus did not exist until He appeared as the historical Jesus, conceived and born as a human.

This Plan...or Logos, as John calls it...was in the beginning with God but *not one single one* of the divine creations were in existence, namely the sun, moon, earth, stars, nor the promises, visitations by angels, visions, dreams, the prophets nor Jesus. *Only the Plan* was there and the whole concept was set in motion when God said the *words*, "Let there be light."

> "For He *spoke*, and it was done; He *commanded* and it stood fast." (Psalm 33:9)

The divine plan is not yet completely manifested...not yet shown...because the saints do not yet fill the earth...but will when they come with Christ at the time He returns to establish His Father's Kingdom.

> "In the beginning was the Word, and the Word was with God and the Word was God...And the Word became flesh and dwelt among us, and we saw His glory, a glory like that of *the first born of the Father*, full of grace and truth." (John 1:1, 14)

Because we now know the true meaning of "logos," a more meaningful and understandable translation might be:

> "In the beginning was God's Plan, and this Plan was with God and the Plan was God. And the Plan became flesh and dwelt among us..."

> "The heavens were made by the word of the Lord and the breath of His mouth." *(Psalm 33:6)*

It was not until centuries later...after the doctrines of the Trinity and of an eternal Jesus were introduced...that LOGOS was translated as Jesus.

To believe that Jesus was with God before creation, and that He was the pattern after which a grown man...Adam...was created, we must stretch our imaginations and believe more:

(1) We would need to believe that He, Jesus, was a grown man when He was with God in Heaven before His birth, as the pattern for the grown man, Adam;

(2) We would need to believe that when it came time for Jesus to come to earth, He had to be reduced from that full grown man to a sperm…God's seed. (God's seed that was to be in Him - 1 John 3:9);

(3) Then, as a Trinitarian, believing that the Holy Ghost is a separate person of the Deity, we would need to believe that God's seed was in *that* one-third of God that was God-the-Holy-Ghost; and that "He" came upon Mary, impregnating her with that seed that grew into Jesus (making Jesus the Son of "God the Holy Ghost" rather than the Son of "God the Father.")

"the Holy Ghost shall come upon thee (Mary)" (Luke 1:35)… "thou shall conceive in thy womb and bring forth a son, and shall call his name Jesus." (Luke 1:31)

(4) We would have to believe that the conception therefrom resulted in a full-term baby which was born flesh and blood;

(5) And then, that this baby grew to be a man *again.* (1Corinthians 15:21; 1 Timothy 2:5)

How simple was the *True* doctrine. Through the *Power of God*, Mary became pregnant with God's Son. God said Jesus was His Son! Jesus said He was God's Son! Why can't we believe them? Until after Jesus' birth, God was never referred to as Father. While He had been the Father of His created son, Adam, God had not "fathered" a child before Christ, and was never called "Father" during the centuries covered by the Old Testament.

Words such as "birth" and "conceive" and "begotten" (Matthew 1:18, 20; Luke 1:31, 33 and 35; and Luke 2:21) used to describe Christ's arrival preclude the possibility of a *prior* existence, but the *beginning* of existence.

If a change from one form of existence to another were factual, the words that would have been used would have been words such as "transformed" "became" or "incarnate." In spite of the fact that Trinitarian teachers insist that Jesus was "Incarnate"...the "incarnation of God"...neither of these words appear *anywhere* in the Scriptures!

Other verses used to try to prove the pre-existence of Jesus are:

> "And no man hath ascended up to heaven but He that came down from heaven, even the Son of Man which is in heaven. "(John 3:13)
>
> "For the bread of God is He which cometh down from heaven." (John 6:33)
>
> "I came down from heaven." (John 6:38)
>
> "I am the living bread which came down from heaven." (John 6:51)
>
> "This is the bread which came down from heaven." (John 6:58)
>
> "...if ye shall see the Son of man ascend up where He was before?" (John 6:62)
>
> "Ye are from beneath; I am from above; Ye are of this world; I am not of this world." (John 8:23)
>
> "...with the glory which I (Jesus) had with Thee (God) before the world was." (John 17:5)

John's gospel passages often employ the Old Testament language of theophany (God appearing). A *manifestation* of divine power is referred to as "*God coming down*" and the completion of the theophany is "*God going up*" or ascending.

For examples of this use of theophany, we look at Genesis 11:5, 8-9, wherein God is said to have "*come down*" to see the tower at Shinar, which later became known as the Tower of Babel. Since no one has ever seen God (1 Timothy 6:16) we know that He did not, Himself, come down. He came down by His angels...His messengers...to manifest Himself...to accomplish

His purposes through others. He "scattered them abroad" and "confounded" their language so that they could not continue with the building of this tower which they proposed to build to heaven. But this was not an earthly appearing of God. He did not "*descend*" except by his agents, the angels, or by the use of His Power.

> "I (God) am come down to deliver them out of the hands of the Egyptians." (Exodus 3:8)

We all know the story of Moses being sent to bring the Hebrews out of Egypt. God did not *"come down"* to do that job Himself. He came, *manifested in the person of Moses,* to accomplish His purpose of delivering His people.

"...for the third day the Lord will *come down* in the sight of all the people upon Mt. Sinai..." God did not personally "come down" but *"the Lord descended upon it" in the form of "fire and smoke" and an "earthquake."* (Exodus 19:18)

Just as God did not "come down," neither did Jesus "come down." His origin was heavenly because God was His Father and His teachings were His Father's. (Luke 1:35; John 7:16; 17:14). The things He spoke came from God...

> "I (Jesus) speak to the world those things which I have heard from Him (His Father*).*" (John 8:26, 28)

"Well," you argue "if He only spoke what He heard from His Father, He must surely have resided with the Father in order to get these instructions and commandments."

Jesus learned the things that His Father wanted Him to say and do *by studying the Scriptures*...just as you and I are directed to do. At as early an age as 12, He was sitting in the Temple, asking and answering questions of the teachers. At that early age He was already amazing the teachers with His wisdom. (Luke 2:46-47)

When He said, in the 49th verse of Luke, "I am about my Father's business," surely we can't believe that he was in the temple learning carpentry, the work of His earthly father, Joseph? He was about His heavenly Father's work in His heavenly Father's house...the Temple.

What do we suppose that Jesus was doing in the time between that occasion in the Temple, at age 12, and the time when we hear of him again when He was 30 years old? His mother doubtless had told Him of the circumstances of His birth and He was studying the Scriptures to learn more about who He was; what He was to do with His short life; what He was to teach others; and what was going to happen to Him on the cross and in the grave. All these things that He knew were to come to pass, He tried to tell His disciples but they couldn't understand. No, He did not get verbal instructions from His Father, He found His instructions in the Holy Scriptures...the infallible Word of God.

Jesus was "foreordained before the foundation of the world..." (1 Peter 1:20). Fore*ordained* but not *formed.* Not until His birth to Mary was He in existence.

When Jesus, at His return, is crowned King in God's earthly Kingdom, it will *not* be the reclaiming of a position that He had held in heaven with His Father, but will be a position that He earned by his righteousness on earth as a human being.

The Son will reign with the power and authority of His Father (1 Corinthians 15:24-28). However, this "more excellent name" was obtained by Jesus *by virtue of his personal worthiness*.

> "Thou (Jesus) hast loved righteousness, and hated iniquity; therefore God, even thy God, has anointed thee with the oil of gladness above thy fellows." (Hebrews 1:9)

This verse tells us several things:

(1) That Jesus, by His sinless life, earned the high position bestowed upon Him by His Father;

(2) That God was Jesus' God, and therefore Jesus could not *be* God;

(3) That this *anointing* of Jesus is God's way of notifying Jesus that He (Jesus) was to serve as king in God's Kingdom...was to sit on the throne...but at a future date. This is not unlike the anointing of Jesus' ancestor, David, who was *anointed* king, but did not take His place on the throne for many years after this anointing. (1 Samuel 16:2, 13)

Because Jesus knew the *Scriptures*, He had known that He would sit on His Father's throne, but only after His own death, His resurrection, His ascension to heaven, and *after His return to earth* to claim His church...a church made up of the followers who knew the True Gospel...the saints that would rule with Him.

With recent indications of the nearness of the end times, when Christ will return for His church, it behooves us to put aside our hostility to the challenge of our beliefs, and to search the Scriptures to be certain that we know the *True Gospel* so that we may be a part of God's Kingdom.

THE LIE:
The Devil Is A Spiritual Person Causing Mankind To Do Evil

Many Christian beliefs have been given mysterious and terrifying meanings that challenge the horror movies of Hollywood. One of these beliefs is that of the Devil as a spiritual being that dwells inside of man, causing man to sin; as a demon-type person who leads man into evil; as a fallen angel; or as a horned being with a long pointed tail, dressed in the red color of fire who will greet you upon your arrival in hell.

In fact, *devil* is not a person but a word *describing* a person; *Satan* is not a person but a word *describing* a person; *demon* is not a person, but *disease*; and the *serpent* is not a person, but *a beast of the field*...a creature of the animal kingdom. But all these things symbolize sinful man...are *personifications of sin...are synonyms for human nature!*

DEVIL:

The word *devil* is derived from the Greek word "Diabolos," which translates as the word "devil," but means "false accuser," "calumniator," "as of the flesh," or "slanderer."

"Did I (Jesus) not choose you, the twelve, and one of you
is *a devil*?" (John 6:70)

Jesus was referring to Judas, whom He knew was about to turn Him over to the Jews who would have Him crucified for crimes of which He was not guilty. In this Scripture, the chosen Judas was a "false accuser"...a "diabolos"...a "devil."

> In the King James translation of John 8:44, it is recorded that Jesus said:
> "You are of your *father the devil*, and the desires of your father
> you want to do..."

> But in the Lamsa translation, the same scripture reads:
> "You are of the *father of accusations* and you want to do
> the lusts of your father."

One translator uses the word "devil" and the other, "accusation"... again, a false accuser. Both mean the same thing. If we truly study our Bibles, it will define itself and we can learn the true meaning of its lessons.

Why is it that most of Christendom believes that there is actually a supernatural, powerful, spiritual being that has certain evil control over man...and is, in fact, blamed for all the evil in the world?

Why? Because mankind has always wanted a scapegoat. When God questioned Adam about eating from the tree of Knowledge of Good and Evil, Adam responded to God's question, saying "the woman whom *thou gavest me*"... (blaming God); "*she* gave me the fruit of the tree..." (blaming Eve); Eve blamed the serpent for beguiling her (Genesis 3:12-13); but the serpent had no one to blame...no devil was lurking in the background.

This human need to place blame elsewhere other than with ourselves started at the very beginning of mankind's existence on earth, and it has been the same ever since. Man has to have someone else to blame for his own failures...and thus the invention of a supernatural devil (or Satan or demon).

To believe that there is some supernatural being that follows us around, tempting us to do evil things, assumes that we would not otherwise think of these sins on our own. Not true!

> "...the Lord saw that the wickedness of man was great in the earth, and that every imagination of the thoughts of his heart was evil continually...the earth was filled with wickedness." (Genesis

6:5,11)

We know, if we truly study our Bibles, that no such spiritual being exists. God tells us that there is no outside force that makes us do evil.

> "There is nothing outside of a man...that can defile him... What comes out of a man, *that* defiles a man. For from within, *out of the heart of men*, proceed evil thoughts, adulteries, fornication, murders, thefts, covetousness, wickedness, deceit, lewdness, and evil eye, blasphemy, pride, foolishness. *All these evil things come from within* and defiles a man." (Mark 7:15,18-23) "The wicked is snared in the works of *his own hands*." (Psalms 9:16)

It is clear that our sins are from our own unchecked, sinful nature.

> "...each one is tempted when he is drawn away by *his own desires and entice*"**...**(not by a person called the Devil). "Then, when desire has conceived, it gives birth to sin; and sin, when it is full grown, brings forth death." (James1:14- 15)

Jesus, Himself, was born with a sinful nature (Romans 8:3) so it is not something of which we should be ashamed, but something we must endeavor to overcome, as Jesus overcame. A righteous nature is not innate, but is a nature to be developed through our faith in Jesus and the new life we receive when we are baptized into His Name.

People want to believe there is this supernatural being...immortal ...living throughout time with a role (with God's blessing) of tempting people to fail. But it is God's will that all should be saved. (1 Timothy 2:4) Why would He send some supernatural, sinful force to lead us astray? He wouldn't! And He hasn't! It is man who has invented this devil-person so that he does not have to face his own sinfulness...so he can escape responsibility...so he has someone to whom he can pass the buck.

When we know this...because God tells us that "every thought in man's heart is evil, continually," (Genesis 6:5) we should be able to understand that all the evil things we do, *WE* do!

Those verses of Scripture, telling of Jesus' forty days in the wilderness and stating that the devil tempted Him to save Himself, are the most frequently used to declare that this evil "person" exists. But lets study the verses, Matthew 4:1-11, to know the truth.

> "Jesus was carried away by the Holy Spirit into the wilderness to be tempted by the ***devil.*** So he fasted forty days and forty nights, but at last he was hungry. And the *tempter* drew near and said to Him, if You are the Son of God, command these stones to become bread."

Jesus was, because of His hunger, tempted just as we would have been tempted. While He possessed characteristics of His Father, God, He was also a human being. He was hungry. He had been in the wilderness alone, without food or water for forty days. He was tempted to do what He knew he could do…to turn the stones into bread so that His hunger might be satisfied. But if He had done that, He would have thwarted His Father's will. He knew that His fate was to be God's sacrificial lamb…that He was to die on the cross.

The "devil" of verse one was "the tempter" of verse three and the "adversary" in the verses that followed. It was His own human nature, tempting Him to be delivered from the death He knew He faced. This "devil," this "tempter," this "adversary" represents Jesus' own sinful nature. (Romans 8:3) In His physical condition, after forty days and nights without food or water, we might expect that hallucinations may have given form to the temptations He experienced…seeing Himself on the steeple, for instance. His desire, *as a human being*, would be to survive and He was surely tempted to do so. But His greater desire to do His Father's will overcame that temptation…that adversary…that devil…and He declined.

And then there was LUCIFER:

Christendom for centuries has taught that "Lucifer" is another name for the external, evil devil…an angel who sinned and fell from heaven. Even dictionaries often say that "Lucifer is a name for the Devil." This definition is accepted by most of Christendom …and exhorted by clergy of almost all denominations. But it does not take much study of our Bibles to see that this is another false teaching. The Lamsa translation does not even contain the word "Lucifer." In Strong's Exhaustive Concordance of the Bible...where we go to find out what chapter and verse contains certain words of the Bible...there is rarely an explanatory note. However, in the case of "Lucifer," the note "Title applied to King of Babylon" is inserted to identify Lucifer.

Some wonder at the use of heavenly language to describe worldly things, but this is not uncommon in the Scriptures. While "Heavenly" is a word sometimes used to described those things in God's heavenly Kingdom or God, Himself, it is more often used to describe things such as people in high places (such as kings, emperors or other leaders). It is used, too, to describe nations that have grown large and powerful...governments.

Moon and stars make reference to leaders of a lesser worldly importance.

And earth, or earthly things, more often than not, refer to the people of nations or governments.

> "Sing, O heavens, and be judged O earth, and break out in singing, O mountains!" (Isaiah 49:13)

Here, God has confronted His people and calls on the nation to praise Him and for it's people to be judged. He surely would not be speaking of His heavenly Kingdom. Nor would He be seeking to judge the dirt of the earth...only those who dwell on the earth.

> "Be astonished, O heaven, at this, and tremble and be exceedingly afraid, says the Lord." (Jeremiah 2:12)

Here God is speaking of the nation of Israel. "They have forsaken Me," He says. (verse 13) "Your own wickedness will correct you, and your backsliding will rebuke you." (verse 19)

God is not talking to His heavenly home nor is He saying that the earth, per se, will tremble. This is a warning to Israel (heavens) and its people (the earth) who had deserted Him.

> "Nevertheless, we, according to His promise (of God's Kingdom on earth), look for a new heaven and a new earth." (2 Peter 3:13)

Another false teaching of Christendom is that heaven and earth will be destroyed and that a new heaven and a new earth will be created. God's heaven is perfect. Why would there even be a suggestion that it would be destroyed. The new heaven is not a replacement for God's *heavenly* Kingdom, it is the new Kingdom of God which will be established *on earth* by God's Son at His second coming.

And as for the earth being destroyed, God's word tells us that while generations will pass away, "*the earth abides forever*." (Ecclesiastes 1:4)

Understanding that "heavens" and "earth" are not literally God's residence and the soil of his creation, let's look at the *only place in the Bible* that the name *Lucifer* is mentioned.

> "How art thou fallen from heaven, O Lucifer, son of the morning! How art thou cut down to the ground, which didst weaken the nations!" (Isaiah 14:12)

The word "Lucifer" is from a Latin word meaning "light bearing." The original Hebrew word means "bright star" or "morning star."

The Revised Standard Version reads:
"How are you fallen from heaven, O Day Star, son of Dawn."

The New English Bible:
"How you have fallen from heaven, bright morning star felled to the earth."

And in the Lamsa translation:
"How you are fallen from heaven! Howl in the morning! For you have fallen down to the ground O reviler of the nations."

The danger is not in reading this one verse from one of the various translations…the danger is in reading *only the one verse*, and in not learning the symbolisms used in the Scriptures.

We need only go back to Isaiah 14 verse 4, where God begins to tell Isaiah what message He wants him to give Nebuchadnezzar, king of Babylon. Then he begins to point out the errors made by the king...how he:

Smote God's people without His instruction;
Chastised them in anger;
Persecuted God's people without pity;
Was pompous;
Was a reviler of nations;
Claimed that he would ascend into heaven;
Would exalt his throne above the stars (above the followers of God);
Destroyed his land and slew his people; and
Declared that he would be like the most high God.

After pointing out the faults of Nebuchadnezzar, God described what would happen to him and his kingdom. God would:

Break the sword of this wicked king;
He would fell him like a tree (cut down but the root left);
He would be thrown down to earth (kingdom would fall);
He would make him the laughing stock of other nations, who would ask if this was the man that made the earth to tremble; shook kingdoms; destroyed the cities of the world; and did not free his prisoners;
He would deliver other nations from his rule;
He would send other nations (which he had overthrown) to capture him; and
God promised that ultimately, Nebuchadnezzar would be thrown into his grave, pierced by the sword.

Having obtained an understanding that heavenly language is often used to describe earthly happenings; and to have studied the verses that preceded Isaiah 14:12, let's take another look at that only mention of Lucifer in the Bible.

Lucifer is a word that means "day star" or "morning star" or refers to "brightness." Anyone who has seen the "day star" or "morning star" knows that it rises rapidly; that it stays visible in the sky for only a short time in the early morning; and then vanishes as quickly as it appeared.

Since we now know that God is sending a message to King Nebuchadnezzar, what do we see in this verse?

> "How you are fallen from heaven, O Lucifer, son of the morning star! How you are cut down to the ground, O you reviler of the nations!"

God told Isaiah to take up this proverb *against the king of Babylon* (v.4) and the entire chapter contains the message from God to the king of Babylon, not to some evil, supernatural, spiritual being known to most of Christendom as the Devil.

This Scripture describes how Nebuchadnezzar had been a fast rising star in the kingdoms of the world of that day. He had ascended to that lofty position (referred to as a heavenly place) by the use of force and terror, and he believed that he had done all of this *on his own*, with no help from God. (Isaiah 14:13-14) He had begun to believe that he was like God. (Isaiah 14:14) Nebuchadnezzar's rise was quick, and God was warning him that he would be "brought down" (Isaiah 14:15). His decline would be equally as fast as his rise. And it was.

In the use of heavenly language, God is using the name "Lucifer" to describe Nebuchadnezzar as the "morning star"...the bright light in the sky in the early morning that falls to the earth and disappears from sight.

In verse 4, God instructs Isaiah to "take up this proverb *against the king of Babylon,*" and the entire chapter is devoted to accomplishing that mission. Lucifer is not a fallen angel, accepted by most of Christendom as "the Devil." The Lucifer of the Scripture is king Nebuchadnezzar, symbolized by the "morning star" that rises quickly and falls as suddenly.

Even today, those who climb the ladder of success in their businesses, governments or careers are referred to as "rising stars." So it was in the days of Babylon.

Let us be certain that Lucifer is not another name for a superhuman, evil being called the Devil.

Christ came into the world to destroy the devil. What He came to destroy was sin.

> "*For this purpose* the Son of God was manifested that He might *destroy the works of the devil.*" (1 John 3:8)

How could the death of God's Son possibly destroy the works of a devil-person?

> "He (Jesus) was manifested *to take away sin.*" (1 John 3:5)

Here, in these two verses, we are given the definition of "devil." It is "sin."

Hebrews 2:14-15 tells us that Christ came to destroy the devil; the devil is that which had the power of death; Christ partook of human nature and died in order to destroy the devil; and in doing so, He delivered others from the devil and from death.

Lets analyze the devil in this scripture.

Christ Came to Destroy the Devil:

> "He put away *sin* by the sacrifice of Himself." (Hebrews 9:26)
> "Christ died for our *sins.*" (1 Cor inthians 15:3)
> "His own self bore our *sins* in His own body on the tree." (1 Peter 2:24)
> "He was manifested to take away our *sins.*" (1 John 3:5)

Christ came to destroy the *devil.* And He accomplished that when He took away *sin.* The Scriptures that tell us what Jesus did, must surely tell us that "devil" is just another word for "sin." How could Jesus' death possibly relate to the destruction of a super-human, powerful, spiritual person? If the devil were such a person, Jesus' death would only give the devil *more* power, having taken the Son of God out of the picture. Once we understand that devil is just a word that relates to sin, and that sin comes from within us, Jesus' death is a powerful weapon to defeat and destroy it.

The Devil is That Which Had the Power of Death:

"The wages of *sin* is death" (Romans 6:23)
"By one man (Adam...not a supernatural devil) *sin* entered the world and death by *sin.*" (Romans 5:12)
"The sting of death is *sin.*"(1 Corinthians 15:56)

When Adam disobeyed God, he brought on himself and on all generations to follow him, death. Had he chosen to eat from the Tree of Life, he would have gained everlasting life for himself, and for all that obeyed God after him. Sin was the original cause of death, and from this evidence, it is obvious that *sin* is what Christ came to destroy and the power of death that is in sin. It logically follows that the devil is a synonym for sin. Even when sin had entered the world, there was no mention of a devil, but man did not remain in his "very good" state. We're told in Genesis 6:5 that man developed "evil" inclinations. What caused the change? Not a supernatural devil, but "*sin.*"

Adam, the very first man, blamed God for giving him Eve and then blamed Eve for giving him the fruit of the Tree of Knowledge of Good and Evil. Man has never wanted to accept responsibility for his own sinfulness, and by making sin into a supernatural being and naming it, he is relieved of his own responsibility and given something ...someone...on whom he can blame his own natural, evil conduct.

It has been that way ever since. Man must blame someone else for his sinful nature, so the Devil was *created* as a scapegoat...*not* by God, but *by man*.

Think back to what God tells us about the world when it was first created. He looked upon all that He had made, *"and behold, it was very good."* (Genesis 1:31) This was before the serpent beguiled Eve, and so even the serpent was good. This description of "very good" applied to all of God's created things. Where was the Devil? It did not exist because sin did not yet exist. And even when the early chapters of the Bible, which record how *sin* entered into the world, there is no mention of a supernatural devil.

"The works of the flesh are evident, which are: adultery, fornication, uncleanness, lewdness, idolatry, sorcery, hatred, contentions, jealousies, outbursts of wrath, selfish ambitions, dissensions, heresies, envy, murders, drunkenness, revelries, and the like...those who

> practice such things shall not inherit the Kingdom of God." (Galatians 5:19-21) "...the tongue is a fire and the sinful world a forest..." (James 3:6)

"The works of the flesh" are the works of our human natures, and our tongues are as destructive as a raging fire. When we are endowed with such proclivities, we certainly don't need to try to shift our sins off onto a supernatural devil. If we want to see the devil, we need only to look in our mirrors.

THE SERPENT:

Ah ha, you say. The serpent is just another name for the Devil. But God tells us that the serpent was a beast of the field. It was probably the most intelligent of all beasts, for it had a capacity to think and it could speak. But when it had deceived Eve into disobeying God, this is what God said to it:

> "Because thou hast done this, thou are cursed above all cattle, and above every beast of the field; upon thy belly shalt thou go, and dust shalt thou eat all the days of thy life." (Genesis 3:14)

Even though the word "devil" does not appear in the Old Testament, many insist that the Serpent is the same supernatural, evil instigator as the Devil...in fact, they insist, they are two names for the same "person."

The serpent was the creature in the Garden of Eden that caused Eve to disbelieve God's warning that death would follow if they ate of the Tree of Knowledge of Good and Evil. It was an upright, speaking and thinking creature (probably the most intelligent creature after man) but because of its wrongful actions, God destined it (and all its descendants) to crawl on its belly and eat dust. If it's crawling on its belly, it doesn't fit the description people give to the Devil they believe exists. True, it (not "he" but "it") introduced sin into the world through Adam and Eve, but God tells us that this creature, and all of its descendants, will always be crawling around in the dust. I think we can dismiss it as some supernatural being, living inside of man and causing him to be evil. You will never hear anyone describe this devil in which they believe so strongly, to be a spiritual, superhuman "thing" that crawls on its belly and eats dust. The serpent was, after the time it beguiled Eve and is today, a member of God's animal kingdom that crawls on its belly and eats dust...and it will be that for all the days of its existence.

SATAN:

And then there is Satan (sathan, in Hebrew; Satan in Greek). Another "person" of man's imagination. Translated to English, the word "satanas" means "adversary" or "oppose" or to "set against." This "Satan" can be either good or bad, so it cannot be a super- human person who leads mankind into evil.

The Aramaic "Satan" or "satano" is derived from the word "sta," which means to "slide," to "slip" or to "miss the mark," and applies to one who causes these results or who falls victim to them.

Jesus referred to Judas as a "devil" in some translations of the Bible, in other translations, the word "Satan" is used. Either way, Jesus was not referring to Judas as a supernatural evil being responsible for all evil, but as one who is a deceiver; one who would oppose Him; one who would falsely accuse Him; one who would "slip" and "miss the mark" Jesus had set for him.

When Jesus was about to be crucified, Peter tried to talk Him into saving Himself, but Jesus knew what His Father wanted His fate to be. And He said to Peter: "Get behind Me, *Satan...*" (Matthew 16:23)

Here, Jesus is referring to Peter, calling him Satan. Surely we can't believe that Jesus is calling this man, whom He had chosen to be one of His disciples...to be the leader in establishing His church...a super-natural instigator of evil in all the world.

In the next few words of that same verse, He defines the meaning of the word "Satan" that he used:

" ...you are an *offense* to Me."

He explains that Peter is an "offense" in that he is opposing God's will...explaining to Peter that he is not mindful of the wishes of God.

"Devil," "Lucifer," "Serpent," and "Satan" are all names *man* has given the "evil one."

If you profess to have accepted Jesus as your savior and have the Spirit of God within you to help you in your spiritual life, will you dare say that there is a devil within you, too, that tempts you...that overrides God's power in your life and causes you to sin?

Anyone claiming to be a Christian. . . who has received the Holy Spirit. . . yet says that there is a devil-being (in whatever form) that has supernatural power over man, is saying that *this devil-being is more powerful than God. . .* more powerful than God's Spirit which you profess is dwelling within you. Do you dare to be one who could believe such a thing?

THE LIE:
Sinners Go To Hell When They Die...
And Burn Forever

Having discovered that there is no spiritual, supernatural "Devil," we must surely understand that this leaves us with no "king" to rule over the kingdom of Hell. In fact, if we study our Scriptures carefully, we will learn that there is not even a "deep-in-the-earth" spot where red hot flames leap to greet and torture sinners when they die. Then where and what is Hell?

Hell, like most other terrifying teachings of the clergy, is a word that means something other than what most have been taught to believe. There are three words that have been translated as "hell": in the Old Testament, the Hebrew word "sheol"; and in the New Testament, the words "hades" and "gehenna."

These are all words that have been taught, by the clergy of most denominations, to describe the home of the Devil, below the earth, to which sinful man is expelled at death, to suffer in the leaping flames and to burn throughout all of eternity. Fortunately, these teachings are false.

For anyone who will study the Scriptures continually and earnestly, it will become clear that "heaven" and "hell," while mentioned many times in the Bible, are *not* the eternal abiding places where people hope (or fear) to go at death. But the main error is not in whether there are such places, but whether or not man has an immortal soul that survives and moves on to one of these destinations at his death.

The Lord God formed man of the dust of the ground and breathed into his nostrils the breath of life and man *became* a *living soul.* (Genesis 2:7) The body, made from the dust and energized by the breath of life, *became* a living soul. Reversing the creation process, when God withdraws his life-giving breath, all that is left of the body is dust.

Knowing that there is no consciousness after death, and that God's Kingdom will be on earth at Jesus' return, there is nothing to support a heavenly home for the righteous dead.

Likewise, since "…the dead know not anything…" (Ecclesiastes 9:5) there would be no burning hell to accept the wicked upon their demise.

When Jesus returns, "those who know not God and those who do not acknowledge the Gospel of Jesus Christ, shall be rewarded with *everlasting destruction.*" (2 Thessalonians 1:8,9)

Now that we have learned, through exhaustive study in the chapter entitled *THE LIE: Man Has An Immortal Soul That Survives His Death,* we can address the fallacy of this belief, knowing that man has no immortal part (nor will he have until the return of Jesus Christ) we can move on to the meanings of the words that have been translated as "hell."

The Hebrew word "sheol" was commonly used to describe the abode of the dead (both good and bad). It is, in fact, another word for "grave" or "covered place." The place where the dead *"know not anything…their love, and their hatred, and their envy, is now perished…there is no knowledge, nor wisdom in the grave* (sheol…hell)." (Ecclesiastes 9:5,6,10)

> "For you will not leave my soul in hades, nor will you allow your Holy One to see corruption." (Acts 2:27)

This is quoting King David as he spoke of the descendant that he knew would eventually sit on his throne. He knew that this anticipated descendant would die; that He would be placed in hades…the grave…but he also knew that God would not allow His Son's body to be corrupted. He knew that Jesus would be raised from the grave and that His corruptible body (His mortal body) would put on incorruption (immortality). God would, David knew, raise up the Christ to sit on his throne...and concerning the resurrection of the Christ, that Jesus was not to be left in the grave to deteriorate. (Acts 2:31)

Jesus' mortal body was changed into an immortal body *when God raised Him from the dead*, just as the mortal bodies of those who believe in Christ, *in Truth*, will be changed to immortal bodies when Jesus returns to gather His church.

> *"...The trumpet will sound...and we shall be changed. For this corruptible must put on incorruption, and this mortal shall put on immortality."* (1 Corinthians 15:52,53)

A popular Scripture of those believing and teaching the fiery hell of torment, torture, and eternal burning is 2 Peter 2:4.

> *"For if God did not spare the angels who sinned, but cast them down to hell and delivered them into chains of darkness to be reserved for judgment..."*

This Scripture has reference to a specific circumstance, and the word translated as "hell" in this instance is "tartarus," a different word than those used in other passages. Tartarus, in Greek *mythology*, referred to a subterranean cavern, a pit, into which were cast the wicked.

It is believed by Bible students, that while Peter does not name them, the "angels that sinned" which were spoken of in this Scripture, were in fact, Korah, Dathan and Abiram. The punishment they suffered for having spoken against Moses and for rebelling against God was a unique punishment and is surely that which was described in the verse.

> *"The ground split apart...the earth opened her mouth, and swallowed them up...they went down alive into the pit, and the earth closed upon them; and they perished."* (Numbers 16:31-33)

This description of an earthquake, swallowing up these rebels against God, provides an adequate explanation of Peter's use of the word "tartarus" in this one instance.

The destiny of the wicked...the sinful...the unbeliever, is to *perish.* John 3:16, which gives us the key to eternal life, points out that the alternative is to perish.

> "For God so loved the world that He gave his only begotten Son, that *whosoever believeth* in Him *shall not perish,* but have eternal life."

The teaching that at death, those who are wicked go to a place of eternal suffering, torment and misery...burning through eternity... is contradicted throughout the Bible. To support such teachings, ministers have, for decades, misread the passages about fire.

Admittedly, most have now come to the conclusion that nothing can "burn forever" without being completely consumed ...destroyed...and that the fire spoken of in the Bible is a word used in describing God's judgment.

> "For the Lord, your *God, is a consuming fire."* (Deuteronomy 4:24)

> "For our *God is a consuming fire."* (Hebrews 12:29)

> "The wicked shall *perish*...they shall *consume away."* (Psalm 37:20)

> "Man that...understandeth not, is like the beast that *perish."* (Psalm 49:20)

> "They are dead...therefore hast thou visited and destroyed them, and made all their memory to *perish."* (Isaiah 26:14)

> "They shall be punished with everlasting *destruction..*" (2 Thessalonians 1:9)

> "Like sheep they are laid in the grave (shoel); Death shall feed on them...and their beauty shall be *consumed* in the grave (shoel)." (Psalm 49:14)

> "...them that *perish;* because they received not the love of the *Truth* that they might be saved." (2 Thessalonians 2:10)

The Greek word "hades" (just as the Hebrew word "shoel") means "the grave" or "a covered place."

The other word translated as "hell" is "gehenna," and it is from this word that the idea of a fiery "hell" is derived. In about a half-dozen places in the Bible, the word "gehenna" is used and is translated as "hell." They are Matthew 5:22, 29, 30; 10:28; 18:8-9; 23:15 and 33, Matthew 18:8 and 9 being the most explicit.

> *"And if thy hand offend thee, cut it off; it is better for thee to enter into life maimed, than having two hands to go into hell (gehenna), into the fire that never shall be quenched: where their worms dieth, and the fire is not quenched."* (Matthew 18:8)

In the New King James Version, the word appears "hell," while in the Lamsa translation (from Aramaic) it is "gehenna"...both are the same.

The word "gehenna" comes from the Hebrew "Ge Hinnom," and while it was a geographically located place, it was in the Hinnom Valley just outside the walls of Old Jerusalem, *not* at the center of the earth. It was a place where the residents of the area burned their refuse, the carcasses of dead animals, and where the unclaimed, unburied bodies of dead criminals were thrown as a way of disposing of them.

In order to alleviate the stench, the fires were kept burning continually and the area became synonymous with death and condemnation. The words "Fires that are never quenched" are used to express the nature of divine judgment...a reminder that God's judgement is certain and that nothing can prevent or interfere with the declared judgement of God against those who turn their backs on Him...suggesting "their worm dieth not."

Revelations 20:14 and 21:8 tell us that the "Lake of Fire" is the second death...the death after judgment...eternal death...eternal separation from God.

Many of the pastors and preachers that, at one time, taught "hell-fire and damnation" as the punishment for sin, have softened their sermons (evangelist Dr. Charles Stanley being one), describing it as "the eternal separation from God" that it is. But while they no longer preach those words in their sermons, they still teach (and believe) the existence of the fiery hell they fear.

The final punishment of the wicked is annihilation, destruction, perpetual death, forever cut off from the living. That is what is meant by perishing!

> "I tell you (said Jesus)...unless you repent, you shall all likewise *perish.* (Luke 13:3,5)

The well known Scripture, John 3:16, tells us that Jesus did not come to punish the wicked. The punishment of those who did not accept Christ as their Savior had already been decided. At the time Adam disobeyed God, death…destruction…had been set as the punishment for the wicked.

Jesus came to give eternal life to those who *did* believe in Him…*in Truth.* All others will *perish.*

> "The wicked shall *perish*...they shall consume away." (Psalm 37:20)

> "The soul that sinneth, it shall *die.*" (Ezekiel 18:4)

THE LIE:
Baptism Is Not Essential

Most so-called Christian denominations will preach that while baptism is desirable, it is not essential to salvation. To most, a simple sprinkling of water on the head is sufficient; few immerse converts completely in water; and many of those, feel that this ritual is unnecessary. So first, let us understand what constitutes biblical baptism.

It is *not* the sprinkling of a few drops of water on the head of the person that is professing an acceptance of Jesus Christ. It most certainly is *not* the sprinkling of a child who is too young to have the knowledge upon which to base the belief that is required *before* baptism.

> "If you *believe* with all your heart, you may (be baptized)..." (Acts 8:36-37)

One who understands the Gospel; who believes that Jesus is the Son of God; who knows that He was born, flesh and blood; died on the cross and was resurrected; one who repents of his sins and believes that he, himself, can some day be resurrected, is the candidate for salvation. He then has been instructed by Jesus, Himself, to be baptized. But to believe and to repent come *before baptism.*

> *"Repent and be baptized, every one of you..."* (Acts 2:38)
> *"He who believes and is baptized shall be saved..."* (Mark 16:16)

The baptism spoken of and the baptism in which biblical Believers always participated, was a complete immersion into (and under) water.

The lowering of the Believer under the water, symbolizes Christ's death *and burial* which ended His *mortal* life.

> *"Do you not know that as many as were baptized into Christ Jesus were baptized into His death?...Therefore we were buried with Him through baptism into death, that just as Christwas raised from the dead by the glory of the Father, even so we also should walk in newness of life."* (Romans 6:3-4)

The raising out of the water symbolizes Christ's resurrection to His *immortal* life.

> "Jesus answered, 'Verily, verily, I say unto you, *except a man be born of water...he cannot enter into the Kingdomof God.'"* (John 3:5)

> "Why are you waiting? Arise and be baptized, and *wash away your sins*, calling on the name of the Lord." (Acts 22:16)

Symbolically, the Believer's sins are washed away at his baptism, and he or she is raised from the water to a "new life." To be saved, one must be "born again" and is expected to live the new life in obedience to Christ's teachings.

> "For if we have been united together in the likeness of His death, certainly we also shall be in the likeness of His resurrection." (Romans 6:5)

The believer must change his old life into a new life *in Christ*.

> "For as many of you as were *baptized into Christ* have put on Christ." (Galatians 3:27)

> "For by one Spirit we were all *baptized into one body* (the church)." (1 Corinthians 12:13)

The sprinkling of a few drops of water does not begin to symbolize the death and resurrection of our Lord, nor the washing away of our sins nor the necessary change in our lives that Christ requires. Such sprinkling won't accomplish Christ's commandment to "be baptized," no matter how much more convenient this simple act of sprinkling might be for the churches of today.

The word "baptism" comes from the word, "baptizo," which means to "dip," or "dye," i.e. to immerse completely in a liquid...to "change color." Baptism is a burial, a complete covering.

With the phasing out of the Old Testament law of Moses and the rituals observed in it, there remained *only two ceremonies required of believers.* (Acts 2:41-42)

(1) The ceremony of *baptism*, (Mark 16:16; Acts 2:38, 41) and
(2) The ceremony of the *breaking of bread* (Matthew 26:26-28; Mark 14:22-25; Luke 22:19-20; Acts 2:42; ; 1 Corinthians 11:23-26).

Baptism is an essential element of salvation. Jesus' own words "unless a man be born of water, he cannot see the Kingdom of God" (John 3:5) does not say to me that I have a choice, but that unless I can follow this simple commandment, I will be excluded from God's Kingdom.

In the early days of the church...in the days of the Apostles...there was no such thing as an unbaptized Christian...and for good reason. The Bible *tells* Believers to repent and be baptized, (Acts 2:38) and that he who believes and is baptized will be saved. (Mark 16:16) It is made clear that this is the only method by which we can put ourselves "in Christ" and have Him in us...and if Christ is not in you through baptism, "you are rejected." (2 Corinthians 13:5) "For as many of you as were baptized into Christ have put on Christ." (Galatians 3:27)

Out of millions who inhabited the earth in the days of Noah, he, with his family, entered the ark that God had commanded him to make.

"only eight souls entered into it, and were saved by its floating upon the water. You also are saved in that very manner *by baptism."* (1 Peter 3:20-21)

Jesus tells us that we are His friend *only* if we do everything He commands us to do (John 15:14) and He has commanded us to be baptized as a means of fulfilling righteousness. (Acts 2:38; Mark 16:16)

Not only are Believers to be baptized themselves, but they have been instructed, by Jesus Himself, to go and teach others...to make disciples of all the nations...*baptizing them* in the name of God, of His Son Jesus Christ, and of the Holy Spirit. (Matthew 28:19)

If we share in Christ's death and resurrection through baptism, then, and only then, *"we shall be also in the likeness of His resurrection...we shall also live with Him."* (Romans 6:5,8)

THE LIE:
Homosexuality Is An Acceptable Lifestyle

There are many who call themselves Christians who say "I believe in Jesus and He never explicitly condemned homosexuality, therefore, neither will I."

These are usually those who think that the Old Testament is outdated...no longer applicable to Christians of today. Nothing could be further from the Truth.

The Christ of the New Testament learned everything that He knew from His Father, God, through the Old Testament. He told us many times that He could do nothing but what His Father instructed Him to do...what His Father commanded Him to do. Where do we think these instructions came from? Do we believe that He met with God from time to time to get His orders? No, He got His instruction from the same place that we should be getting ours. From His Father's inspiring Words which were given to, and recorded by, the prophets of the Old Testament.

Though His mother surely told Him about the circumstances of His miraculous birth, Jesus, Himself, referred to the Old Testament in His teachings. It is these Old Testament Scriptures that foretold His coming and taught Him about Himself.

The circumstances of Jesus' birth (Isaiah 7:14; 9:6; ll:1-2); the nature of His relationship with God (2 Samuel 7:14); the prophesy regarding His suffering and false conviction (Isaiah 53:3-9; 63:3; Jeremiah 33:15); the details of His crucifixion (Psalms 16:10; 22:11, 16, 18; 34:20; 69:4, 9, 21; 78:2; Zechariah 11:12; 35:5; 49:8); His resurrection (Psalms 49:15); and His purpose thereafter (Psalms 2:9; 45:6; 72:4, 5, 9, 11; Isaiah 2:2-3;6:9-10; 9:7; 22:22; 35:5; 49:8) *were all foretold in the Old Testament.*

The Old Testament is where Jesus learned all that He knew. It is where He found out what He was to do with His life; what His purpose was; and what His fate would be, both earthly and heavenly.

God's word does not change because we want it to. He told us in His own words: "I am the Lord, *I change not.*" (Malachi 3:6) We are not True Christians if we reject God's Word. Christendom, today, tries to make God's Word suit the contemporary culture of the day, when it should be trying to change the culture to bring it into compliance with God's Word.

Because homosexuality is acceptable in this *world*, which is growing more immoral each day, Christendom feels it must re-evaluate and re-interpret God's Word to make this sin of homosexual behavior acceptable in His church.

But homosexuality was acceptable in the *culture* at the time God spoke against it, making it clear that it was not acceptable to God. Time has not changed that. Fourteen of the first fifteen emperors of Rome were homosexuals and against this background, God forbade homosexuality for *His* people.

Since God never changes, and Jesus received all of His commands from God, can we reasonably believe that Jesus would abolish His Father's commands regarding such a lifestyle? Just because there is no record of Jesus having specifically rejected the lifestyle of homosexuals does not...and cannot...be interpreted to mean that He accepted it, knowing what His Father had said.

There was then, and there is now, a blatant tension between God's Word and the conduct of the world around us...and it will always be that way. It is the nature of man...the evil nature of man (Genesis 8:21)...to reject God's Words or to try to make them fit his own lifestyle and lusts, for we are told that "every thought in man's heart is evil, continually." (Genesis 6:5) Though those who practice such conduct will make life miserable for those who speak God's Word (Galatians 4:29), in the end, the carnally minded are the ones who will be denied acceptance into the Kingdom of God. (Romans 8:6)

> "...you dishonor the Word of God for the sake of the tradition which *you* have established,"(Mark 7:13) "and they worship me in vain when they teach the doctrines of the *commandments of men.*" (Mark 7:7)

We are told in Genesis 2:18-24, that woman was created as a helper to man...a counterpart or mate. She was not designed just to be a receptacle for the overflow of his sexual activity. God created the anatomy of man and woman to compliment each other...to fit together *for a purpose*. God describes the homosexual as "leaving the *natural use of the woman*." (Romans 1:27)

Men were not designed by their Creator to have intercourse with other men. Such conduct rips tissue and seems intended to spread disease. This should be apparent by the spread of devastating diseases such as AIDS, which has grown to epidemic proportions since the spread of the homosexual lifestyle. This, if nothing else, should convince us that homosexuality is not a conduct of which our God approves.

Although some gays claim that they are born that way...profess to be "true," as they put it. But there has been no proof that either men or women are "born" gay. But for the sake of argument, let us assume that some are. This does not make the conduct acceptable in God's eyes. Everyone is born with a sinful nature. Even Jesus came into the world with the same sinful nature as other men (Romans 8:3), but sinful *nature* and sinful *conduct* are two different things. Jesus struggled and overcame the temptations He faced and we are taught that we must experience similar struggles against *our* sinful natures... our evil hearts...in an attempt to overcome the temptations and lust of the flesh. (Romans 3:10; 5:12; Galatians 3:22; 5:17; James 3:8)

For those who argue that Old Testament laws were abolished by Jesus and thus are no longer applicable, we need only look at 1 Corinthians 6:9 and 1 Timothy 1:10 (both in the *New Testament*), which tell us that there is no place in God's kingdom for "men who lie with males." Jesus did not sanction sin because the written laws of Moses had been superseded by His own teachings.

While the Law of Moses was ended by Christ's sacrificial crucifixion, it doesn't follow that God's moral principles changed as well. God did not see homosexuality as an "abomination" the day before Christ's death, then the day after, changed His mind about it. He told us "I am the Lord, I do not change." (Malachi 3:6)

If those who are *True* Christians do not stay separate from those who are homosexuals...those whom God has told us have no place in His Kingdom...those Christians will suffer the same judgment, the same eternal death...the same fate as their gay friends. (Romans 1:32; Proverbs 17:15)

Our world is getting more and more like the Sodom that God destroyed because of the great sins of its people...primarily the homosexuality of that population. (Revelations 18:4)

That is not to say that Christians are justified in being homophobic...haters of homosexuals. Gays must be treated just as those who might be addicted to alcohol or drugs or heterosexual sex. Christians should encourage them to seek whatever help it takes to overcome the addiction of homosexuality, and to provide them with spiritual support in their attempt to "kick" the habit...to teach them that any sin can be forgiven with repentance. (1 Corinthians 6:11)

"When God condemned homosexuality, He was only talking about homosexual prostitutes," argue our homosexual church population.

But what God said was "Thou shalt not lie with mankind as with womankind; it is an abomination." (Leviticus 18:22) When God spoke, He was speaking to *His people*...all of them! He was not lecturing a group of prostitutes, and nothing in the Scriptures supports the homosexuals' position on this issue.

The dis-fellowshipping of someone who has committed such a sin...the refusal to worship with them...is the New Testament punishment for sins that would have been "worthy of death" under Old Testament law. In those early days of the Hebrews, homosexual acts were punishable by death...and in the early days of the Christians, the participants were excluded from the fellowship of God's people, *and so they should be today.*

Christians who sanction such conduct, and who fellowship with those who practice these pervert acts, are themselves as guilty as those who actually participate in the acts and are subject to condemnation. (Romans 1:32; Proverbs 17:15)

All *True* Christians accept the Bible as the inspired word of God. If we do that and reject the messages It gives us...as most of Christendom does...then we are rejecting God, and we need to turn our lives around.

Many Christian denominations...the Lutherans for one...have a list of homosexual clergy. Most denominations welcome active homosexuals into their congregations. In the Roman Catholic church, it is obvious from the constant news reports, that homosexuality runs rampant in its clergy. Not only homosexuality, but Pederasty (sex with minor boys) as described in Joel 3:3... and the headlines rang out the same accusations against Mormon leaders a few years ago, though the "news" reports were primarily confined to Utah.

What does all this say about so-called Christian churches? It says that they are *apostate* churches...that they will be excluded from God's Kingdom.

Those who believe that any homosexuality is acceptable to God...and therefore should be acceptable to God's church...simply refuse to search the Bible for God's Truth.

Even with a clear conscience as to their conduct, homosexuals cannot rightfully join the church. Man is not judged by what *he, himself,* believes of himself. Man is judged by his reaction to the Word of God! (John 12:48) Our Lord Jesus, Himself, warned us to "take heed that the light which is in you is not darkness"...that man is to be careful not to believe that he is right when he is wrong. (Luke 11:35) Our Bibles will tell us the difference.

The person who does a superficial reading of the Bible can be deceived by its words. Such casual reading...with the assistance of deceitful "Christian" clergy...will lead to belief in a false gospel. (2 Corinthians 11:4; Galatians 1:6-7)

Unless Christians devote themselves, *wholeheartedly*, to the study of God's Word, they will fail to find the Truth and God will deceive them and allow their apostate beliefs to continue and grow.

> *"God gave them up to uncleanliness through the lusts of their own hearts, to dishonour their own bodies between themselves...For this cause God gave them up unto vile passions; for even their women did change the natural use into that which is against nature: and likewise also the men, leaving the natural use of the woman, burned in their lust one toward another; men with men committing shameful acts, and receiving in themselves the recompense of their error...God gave them over to a debased mind to do those things which are not fitting."* (Romans 1:24-32*)*

God designed us to make free-will decisions, and once we have done so, He confirms them. When men lust after men...and women lust after women...and then justify those lusts, God does something to their minds to lead them in the way of their own desires. Romans 1:29-31 points out that homosexuality leads to other sins such as envy, murder, inventors of evil things, maliciousness, etc. The Bible makes the connection between homosexuality and other crimes.

The men of Sodom...nearly all of them...both young and old...who tried to force their way into Lot's home...were homosexuals who wanted to commit sexual acts upon Lot's male guests. They threatened more serious crimes against Lot if his guests were not turned over. God destroyed the entire city with volcanic lava, engulfing them all. (Genesis 19:4-8)

In Judges 19: 22-28, we are told of another male house guest who was demanded as a sexual partner, the invaders committing other crimes when they were denied sexual access to the visitor.

Six of the seven top male serial killers in the United States were gay...(and if the reports given against the two accused Beltway Snipers is true, make that eight out of nine)...as were many of the concentration camp operators.

> *"If a man lies with a male as he lies with a woman, both of them have committed an abomination; they shall both die."* (Leviticus 20:13)

...and not only the homosexuals, "*but those who associate with them.*" (Romans 1:32)

This is the final death...the one that separates man from God for eternity.

> *"Do you not know that the wicked shall not inherit the Kingdom of God? Be not misled; neither the immoral...nor men who lie with males...shall inherit the Kingdom of God"* (1 Corinthians 6:9-10)

The clergy of today has retreated from the moral teachings of the Bible, defining immorality as "mature freedom" when, in fact, they are leading their congregations into a downward spiral to destruction.

The True Christian church is expected, by God, to be the beginning of His everlasting Kingdom. Anything that will be prohibited from His *future* Kingdom must be prohibited, also, from His church *now*.

Our association or disassociation with (or our approval or disapproval of) homosexuals is a salvation issue.

THE LIE:
All Who Call Themselves Christians Should Worship Together

For the past decade or so, the various denominations have been gathering together as one congregation, advocating the joint worship of all Christian denominations. Even the Roman Catholic church (which heretofore had considered itself above the others, and believed it possessed the only true faith) has discovered that this joint-worship can provide a potential for increasing its already astounding numbers, its tremendous wealth and its astronomical power in the religious community. "Ecumenical" is the word given to this movement to join together faiths that do not necessarily have the same beliefs.

The affirmation that the Bible is the Word of God and that a belief in God's Son, Jesus Christ, is the condition for salvation is universal in the Christian community. While almost every household in the United States has a Bible...and many have more than one...relatively few actually read this perpetual best-seller and even fewer study it to see what it says to those who call themselves Christians.

A few years ago, Pope John sponsored a day of prayer for peace, inviting leaders of the world religions...Catholics, Orthodox, World Council of Churches, the Sheiks, Muslims, Buddhists, Confucians, and a variety of African religions. "Welcome home!" was the greeting these leaders met on arrival.

Did you notice that the list of invited participants did not include representatives of God's chosen people, the Jews? Nor, apparently, were evangelical Christians who support Israel.

Whenever and wherever the participants gathered, including the famous Basilica of St. Francis, all of the crosses and other Christian objects had been removed, and the name of Jesus Christ was omitted entirely from all its worship services.

Biblically, such a gathering called by the Pope (who professes to be the head of Christianity itself) should have called for headlines around the world to scream out the occasion. But the media saw nothing worth much time and space. But those who know their Bibles saw the fulfilling of the prophesied "One World Religion of Biblical Prophesy," *the false religion which denies the authority of the Scriptures and will persecute those who hold to Scripture.*

(2 Peter 2:1; 1 John 4:1; Revelation 3:1)

While the published rules of some of the well-known denominations (Lutheran, Baptist, Methodist, etc.) make it clear that such "togetherness" is not acceptable, they nevertheless attend such functions and their congregations welcome this ecumenical trend, attending these joint worship services whenever the opportunity presents itself. So many, in fact, have wandered from their former churches that now there is a *denomination* called the "Ecumenical Church," and even more recently, referred to as "Churchianity" rather than "Christianity." Perhaps the attraction to those of today's lax culture is the fact that these churches do not set forth decided doctrinal beliefs nor are there many requirements of their members, behavioral or otherwise. Many such churches do not even keep membership lists.

So what does this Bible (that Christians profess to believe in) tell us about worshiping with "unbelievers."

"An *UNBELIEVER!* Who are you calling an unbeliever?"

You cannot have salvation, says the Catholic Church, if you do not accept it's doctrines, and therefore, if you do not accept it's doctrines, you are an "unbeliever."

The Lutheran Church sets forth it's requirements for salvation, and if you do not accept them, you are assured that you cannot be saved. Therefore, not accepting the doctrines set forth by that church, labels you an "unbeliever."

Most denominations have their own doctrines...their own set of rules and regulations establishing the right-of-passage into God's Kingdom. Not to accept those doctrines makes you, in their eyes, an "unbeliever."

So I ask again, what does the Bible say about worshiping with unbelievers?

It says, *"DON'T!"*

O. K., what is an *unbeliever*? It is one who does not believe the gospel *as it was taught by Paul (and the other Apostles).* If he doesn't believe in *that* gospel, *"let him be eternally condemned.*" (Galatians 1:9) So anyone who believes in any false gospel...in a false doctrine...is necessarily an unbeliever. To be saved, we need to keep the doctrines taught by the disciples.

> "If anyone teaches a different doctrine, he knows nothing."(1 Timothy 6:3-4)

If we believe that all that *profess* to be Christians are "in Christ"...we are saying that they are our Christian brothers and sisters. But if we know that their doctrines are incorrect, where does that put us?

While we are generally told to leave judgment up to God, we are not only given the right to judge our Christian brothers and sisters, we are *commanded* to do so (Matthew 18:15-16). And if they do not abandon their false beliefs, we are not to associate with them. (Matthew 18: 17)

If these people are *not in Christ...*are not our brothers and sisters in Christ...they are unbelievers and are unclean in God's eyes. In that case we have another commandment...to *"be ye separate"* and to touch not the unclean thing...to *"come out from among them and be ye separate."* (2 Corinthians 6:17) Second Corinthians 6:14 instructs us not to be yoked with unbelievers.

Unfortunately, a great majority of those who call themselves Christians have no idea what the beliefs of their denominations are...in fact, don't really know what *their own individual beliefs are*. They are happy to sit in church week after week and let their pastors, preachers, evangelists, priests, and others tell them what the Bible says. If it is pleasing to them, they accept it. If it displeases them, they either reject it or move on to another church where the emphasis is put elsewhere. This is not surprising to those who study their Bibles, as the Scriptures...written thousands of years ago...warned us that this would happen...that even those in the church would turn away from the Truth and teach false doctrines.

The Bible tells us, clearly, that God's Word is *Truth* (John 17:17)... and that our salvation is conditioned on believing the *Truth.* (2 Thessalonians 2:12) We cannot expect to enter into God's Kingdom without agreeing on what the Bible says. When we agree to disagree on what it tells us, we reduce the Truth to a matter of opinion and render the Word of God ineffective.

Reading these and many other Scriptures, we can see that one can only enter the Kingdom of God in *Truth.* Since there can be only *one Truth,* how can congregations of the more than 2,000 religious groups in the world today, with their varying beliefs, expect to obtain salvation?

> "...because they did not receive the love of the *Truth*... all who did not believe the *Truth*...might be damned." (2 Thessalonians 2:10,12)

We will not be excused for believing a false doctrine just because our "preacher" told us it was true. We are given the personal responsibility of studying the Scriptures for ourselves and in searching out its messages.

If we *cannot,* without hesitation, say *"I know the Truth of the gospel of the Kingdom of God and of Jesus Christ,"* then we had better start searching for it.

If we *can* express such a belief, then we had better start trying to teach it to others, since turning a sinner from the error of his ways will save that sinner from eternal death, and will cover a multitude of our own sins. (James 5:19-20)

Not everyone will accept the Truth, no matter how hard an attempt is made to change their false beliefs. And if they will not learn the Truth, then God will give them over to "strong delusion that they should believe a lie." (2 Thessalonians 2:10-11)

To marry someone...or to worship with someone...who does not have the same beliefs, is to be "unequally yoked." Such is mingling believers with unbelievers; like mingling light with darkness; like trying to mingle Christ with sin; like mixing the temple of God with idols. (2 Corinthians 6:14-16)

> "Wherefore come out from among them, and *be separate*...and I will receive you, and will be a Father to you, and you shall be my sons and daughters, said the Lord." (2 Corinthians 6:17-18)

When Christ comes for His church, He will raise, and give immortality, first to those that are "dead in Christ," after which he will change from mortal to immortal those that are "*alive* in Christ." (1 Thessalonians 4:16-17) What does it mean to be "in Christ"?

To be in Christ, one must have been baptized into Christ's name *after* knowing the *Truth* of the gospel and repenting of past sins. Those who accomplish this are then brothers and sister of Christ...children of God. It is when Christians become brothers and sister that they become responsible for one another. They are then a family and have been instructed to watch after...and watch over...each other and to guide each other in the way of Truth. If one begins to wander, it is up to his or her brothers or sisters to lead him or her back to the Truth. (Matthew 18:15-17) A true Christian is responsible for all other True Christians and when they meet together, are instructed by Jesus, Himself, to break bread and share the wine in memory of His death. (1 Corinthians 11:24-25)

So what is this Truth in which we are required to believe? It is the *Gospel of the Kingdom of God and Jesus Christ*...the Gospel and the Jesus that was taught by the Apostles (1 John 2:24) "...continue steadfastly in the Apostles' gospel..." (Acts 2:42)

Practically none of the so-called Christian denominations today believe or teach the Apostles' gospel, but expound to their congregations the man-made gospel that was developed by the Roman church hundreds of years after the death of the Apostles and imposed on Christianity as a means of appeasing the idolaters in the days of Constantine. Unfortunately, those that pulled away from the Roman church to establish other denominations failed to leave behind those false doctrines but adopted them as their own. This should not surprise us. We were warned of it. "And many will follow their destructive ways, because of whom the way of Truth will be blasphemed." (2 Peter 2:2)

We are told, in 1 John 5:5-8, of the beliefs that establish *Truth*. We must believe in God…that He *begot* Jesus; we must believe that Jesus is His Son, *begotten* of God; we must have the Spirit of God within us after experiencing the water of *baptism*; and we must know that Christ died…shed his blood…for us and was raised from the dead, just as those who believe the Truth shall be raised. *We must be born again* "not just of water but of water and blood."

> "There is *one* Lord, *one* Faith, *one* baptism, *one* God and Father of all…" (Ephesians 4:5-6)

Please note that the instruction calls for one *Faith*…not *one Gathering of churches*.

Those who claim to be Christians, but who hold doctrines that are openly opposed to clear Bible teaching, are "in darkness" and we are to "have no fellowship with the unfruitful works of darkness." (Ephesians 5:11) "Wherefore, come out from among them, and *be ye separate*, saith the Lord…" (2 Corinthians 6:17)

Such a direction from the Lord, Himself, should warn us that worshiping together with just anyone who *calls* himself a Christian is unacceptable.

The breaking of bread and the sharing of wine is a memorial service…referred to as "communion" or "fellowship"… to remind us of Christ's death and bloodshed. This service should only be shared by those who share a common understanding of the *Truth*. "Communion" is, in fact, a combination of two words…"common" and "union."

1 John 1:2,3 explains the necessity of believing the gospel taught by the Apostles so that "you also may have fellowship with us."

This fellowship should bind us together in "singleness of heart." (Acts 2:46) Only those who have been properly baptized into Christ (after knowing and believing the *Truth*) are in a position to participate, and should not share or worship with anyone who holds another belief.

> "I write to you...so you may know how you ought to conduct yourself in the church of the living God, the pillar and foundation of the *Truth*." (1 Timothy 3:15)

> "Examine yourselves, whether you are in the same faith; heal yourselves..." (2 Corinthians 13:5)

Doctrine is important to our salvation. We become, or respond to, the basic gospel we believe, and cannot live a pure life if we are not "pure in the doctrine." (Philippians 1:27) There is only one True church (Ephesians 1:23) which is based on belief in "*one* hope, *one* God, *one* Baptism and *one* faith." (Ephesians 4:4-6) It is impossible to hold to the *True Faith* while worshiping with other religious organizations who do not. "One faith" does not mean the gathering into an ecumenical relationship with those of separate and different beliefs.

> "You were doing so well. Who confused you that you should not obey the *Truth*." (Galatians 5:7)

Even those in our own denomination must remain in the Truth. If brothers and sisters persist in false teachings, we are told that it is necessary to formalize the cessation of the fellowship that has occurred. (Matthew 18:15-17)

The *Gospel* is the Good News of the Kingdom of God and Jesus Christ. The beliefs of most of Christendom is of a Kingdom that will be in heaven (though the Bible assures us it will be on earth) (Acts 1:9,11; Revelation 5:10); of the immortality of the soul (rather than that the dead will sleep in death until Jesus returns to resurrect them as the Scriptures tell us) (Psalm 6:5; Acts 2:29, 34); on the belief of a devil-person to whom they attribute powers as great as those of God (even though the Bible assures us that devil is not a person but a word meaning adversary, and that all evil comes from within man, himself) (Mark 7:18-23).

But most importantly, they believe that Jesus is God...that God came down in the person of His own Son rather than being the begotten Son that both Jesus and God said He was. "Jesus is *only a man*..." (John 10:33) How can He be God? "God is *not a man*..." (Hosea 11:9). How can He be Jesus?

What could be more evil than to drag the incorruptible God down, turn Him into the corruptible man that Jesus was, and to worship Him as God? (Romans 1:23-25)

The doctrines of Jesus Christ are His teachings, and His teachings clearly dispel all of the beliefs held by most of Christendom. That being the case, how can we even suggest that those who embrace such doctrines are believers? And if we know that they are not Believers, we must stay separate...and certainly we must not break bread with them. The judgment of God condemns not only those who practice evil things against Him, but those who associate with those who practice them. (Romans 1:32)

Those churches that teach the doctrines of the Trinity, the immortal soul, a personal devil, fiery hell, God's eternal Kingdom in heaven, and other doctrines contrary to Bible teachings, have no place in the congregation of those who worship in *Truth.*

SUMMARY

Jesus instructed His Believers to spread the Gospel of the Kingdom of God, not as paid preachers, but as believers. But instead of the selfless service and devoted personal dedication He expects from His followers, ambitious men have turned their religions into careers. Though we were warned to preach willingly, *but not for money*, (Peter 5:2), this is a far cry from what is happening in the churches of today.

The clear teachings and doctrines of our Lord, Jesus Christ, have been corrupted, manipulated and distorted in church councils, questioned in religious circles, and revamped to conform to the designs of churchmen and to the demands of their congregations.

Rather than faithful spiritual individuals teaching the gospel, hierarchies were formed to rule over and direct Bible teachings. The stake upon which Christ was sacrificed was changed into a cross which became the symbol of the apostate church that He will reject.

Many will not experience the salvation they have been assured is theirs, because they cling to cherished and false doctrines, fed to them by a deceitful clergy.

They do not "search the scriptures to see if what they say is true" and are hostile to any who question the doctrines they hold.

Jesus said that He was the Son of God. Why can't we believe Him?

"...he who does not believe the Son shall not see life (eternal) but the wrath of God abides on him." (John 3:36)

Many of my own loved ones can open their Bibles, look at the words "Son of God" and see nothing but "God the Son," closing their eyes to the Truth. But Jesus said that *"in vain they worship Me, teaching as doctrine the commandments of men...making the Word of God of no effect through your traditions which you have handed down."* (Mark 7:13) The man-made commandments and the church traditions encompassed in the Trinity doctrine have made the Word of God of no effect.

Not being susceptible to learning, they will never *know* the Truth and those who seek to enter through improper doctrine will be cast into darkness and, at judgment, will be a participant in the chorus of the gnashing of teeth. (Matthew 22:13)

I have been through the Scriptures, searching for a single verse that even *implies* that an *oral statement of belief* in Jesus Christ will save you...much less that such a statement assures you of permanent salvation. I find none.

Throughout the Bible we are told...over and over again...that we *must obey Jesus*; *must be baptized*; *must live our lives as He lived His to the best of our abilities*; *must follow His commandments*; and *must be steadfast to the end*, if we expect to enter into God's Kingdom in the last days. Salvation is an unconditional gift? Where are we told that?

We know that Jesus was God's "indescribable gift." (2 Corinthians 9:15) But you obtain salvation by embracing that gift in the way that God dictates.

We are told that God's Spirit within us is a gift (1 Timothy 4:4; 2 Timothy 1:6), but we must have accepted Jesus as the Son of God and as our Savior and be baptized into His name before we receive that Spirit.

The "message of salvation" was sent by God. (Acts 13:26) Jesus was that message. "The salvation of God has been sent to the Gentiles" (Acts 28:28), but we must reach out and embrace it in *Truth*. Yes, it is a *free* gift...(Romans 5:18) but it is *not* unconditional.

Those who are in the congregations of churches that are growing in numbers (numbers of churches throughout the world and numbers of members in those churches) should stop and wonder about what their clergy is teaching. The fantastic numbers being bragged about in the various denominations should set their congregations to searching their Bibles to see if this, in itself, might not be a sign that they are entering "the wide gate"... "the wide way"...that leads to destruction. For we know that "narrow" is the gate...and "narrow" the way...that leads to everlasting life.

> "Enter by the narrow gate; for wide is the gate and broad is the way that leads to destruction...because narrow is the gate and difficult is the way which leads to eternal life...*and there are few who find it."* (Matthew 7:13-14)

> "Strive to enter in through the narrow door; for I say to you, many will seek to enter in and *will not be able."* (Luke 13:24)

> "Many are called, but *few are chosen."* (Matthew 22:14)

Those who teach that Jesus is God, are not teaching the Jesus that the Apostles taught. One who "preaches another Jesus whom we (the Apostles) have not preached...are false apostles and deceitful workers, posing as apostles." (2 Corinthians 11:3-4)

Paul gave the earlier followers of Christ a warning: "...just as the serpent, through his deceitfulness, misled Eve, so your minds shall be corrupted from the sincerity that is in Christ." (2 Corinthians 11:3) "What is highly esteemed among men" (which the doctrine of the Trinity *is*) *is disgusting in the presence of God."* (Luke 16:15)

God is the original...Jesus is the image of that original. The Jesus of the Trinity, is not the Jesus that the Apostles taught, and they that teach such false doctrines, and those that follow after them, are destined to eternal separation from God.

"We (Paul and Timothy) write nothing to you (the church at Corinth) except those things which you know and *understand."* (2 Corinthians 1:13) No one, not even the church that invented it, can understand the doctrine of the Trinity.

To those who worship God with their mouth…their lips…but have removed their hearts far from Him and those whose reverence toward Him is taught by the "*precepts and doctrine of men*," God promises that the wisdom of these wise men shall perish." (Isaiah 29:13-14)

God wants us to IMITATE…*not* to INNOVATE. The oft heard phrase "I did it my way" is not what God wants to hear. He wants us to do it *His* way! He has given us a free will with which to choose or reject the Truth. If we persist in clinging to long-held, deeply-rooted, but incorrect beliefs, God will not only allow us to do that but will harden the hearts of whom He pleases, allowing the wrong belief to lead to destruction. (Romans 9:18)

Peter warned of this internal foe (2 Peter 2:1-3); Jude exposed their characteristics (Jude 4); Paul strove with them (Galatians 1:6-12, 2 Corinthians 11:13); and John labeled them "anti Christ," identifying their key doctrines as error (1 John 4:1-3). The universal church system destroys the authority of Almighty God. For salvation, those within that system must "*come out of her, that ye be not partakers of her sins, and that ye receive not of her plagues.*" (Revelation 18:4)

We have been assured that all who change the image of the incorruptible God for an image of corruptible man (which Jesus was) and worship him as God; who change the truth for lies; who worship the created rather than the Creator;…all will be condemned by God and "*not only them but those who associate with them.*" (Romans 1:32)

Our salvation is conditional on worshiping God in *Truth.* (John 4:24) *Find that Truth before it is too late!*

ADDENDUM

Soul: As is explained in Encyclopedia Britannica, the soul is "the functioning unit of an individual, not some part of him." "In other words," it continues, the soul is "the living, mortal person and not a homesick visitor from the eternal region." But we need only to compare the various translations of the *Bible* to get the meaning of "soul." The Bible defines itself, if we truly seek its definition. Here are approximately 350 verses from the Bible which use the word "soul" in one translation, and a different word, which means the same thing as "soul," in another translation.

Verses marked (KJ) - taken from the King James Version;
Verses marked (NKJ) - taken from the New King James;
Verses marked (L) - taken from the Lamsa Translation;
Verses marked (NIV) - taken from the New International Version;
Verses Marked (TLB) - taken from The Living Bible;
Verses marked (RV) - taken from the Revised Standard Version;
Verses marked (D) - taken from the Diaglott (New Testament)

This author hereby wishes to express her great appreciation to those who hold the publishing rights and/or copyrights to these valuable translations of God's Word for their permission to use them here.

To Thomas Nelson, Inc., 501 Nelson Place, Nashville, TN 37214, for permission to quote from the King James Version, The New King James version, and the Revised Standard Version;

To A. J. Holman Company and Harper Collins Publishers, 10 E. 53 Street, 20th Floor, New York, N. Y. 10022, for permission to quote from the

Lamsa translation;

To the Zondervan Corporation, 5300 Patterson, S. E., Grand Rapids, MI 49530 for permission to use quotes from NIV. Scriptures taken from the HOLY BIBLE, NEW INTERNATIONAL VERSION (R), Copyright (C) 1973, 1978, 1984 by International Bible Society. Used by permission of Zondervan Publishing House. All rights reserved. The "NIV" and "New International Version" trademarks are registered in the United States Patent and Trademark Office by International Bible Society. Use of either trademark requires the permission of International Bible Society;

To Tyndale House Publishers, Inc., 351 Executive Drive, Wheaton, IL 60189, for permission to quote from The Living Bible.

"...and man became a *living soul.*" (KJ)
"...and man became a *living being*." (L, NKJ, NIV, RV)
"...and man became a *living person...*" (TLB)
(Genesis 2:7)

"...and *my soul* shall live because of thee." (KJ)
"... and that *I* may live because of you..." (NKJ)
"...and *my life* shall be spared because of you." (L, NIV, RV)
"...and spare *my life...*" (TLB)
(Genesis 12:13)

"...that *soul* shall be cut off from his people..." (KJ)
"...that *person* shall be cut off from his people..." (NKJ, L, RV)
"...any...*male*...shall be cut off from his people..." (NIV)
"...*anyone*...shall be cut off from his people..." (TLB)
(Genesis 17:14)

"...and *my soul* shall live." (KJ, NKJ)
"...*my life* will be spared." (L, NIV)
"...and *my life* will be saved..." (TLB, RV)
(Genesis 19:20)

"...that *my soul* shall bless thee before I die." (KJ, L)
"...that *my soul* may bless you..." (NKJ)

"...that *I* may give you my blessing before I die." (NIV, TLB)
"...that *I* may bless you before I die..." (RV)
(Genesis 27:4)

"...that *your soul* may bless me." (KJ, L, NKJ)
"...so that *you* may give me your blessing." (NIV)
"...so that *you* will bless me..." (TLB)
"...that *you* may bless me..." (RV)
(Genesis 27:19)

"...that *my soul* shall bless thee..." (KJ, L)
"...that *my soul* may bless you..." (NKJ)
"...that *I* may give you my blessing." (NIV)
"...*I* will...bless you with all my heart..." (TLB)
"...that *I* may eat...and bless you..." (RV)
(Genesis 27:25)

"...so that *thy soul* may bless me..." (KJ, L)
"...that *your soul* may bless me..." (NKJ)
"...so that *you* may give me your blessing." (NIV)
"...so that *you* can give me your finest blessing..." (TLB)
"...that *you* may bless me..." (RV)
(Genesis 27:31)

"...And his *soul* clave unto Dinah..." (KJ)
"...his *soul* was strongly attracted to Dinah..." (NKJ)
"...And his *soul* longed for Dinah..." (L)
"...His *heart* was drawn to Dinah..." (NIV)
"...*He* fell deeply in love with her..." (TLB)
"...and *his soul* was drawn to Dinah..." (RV)
(Genesis 34:3)

"...the *soul* of my son..." (KJ, L, NKJ, RV)
"...*my son* has his heart set...(NIV)
"...*my son* is truly in love with your daughter..." (TLB)
(Genesis 34:8)

"...as *her soul was departing*..." (KJ, L, NKJ, RV)

"...as *she was dying*..." (NIV)
"...and with *Rachel's last breath*..." (TLB)
(Genesis 35:18)

"...we saw the anguish of *his soul*..." (KJ, L, NKJ)
"...we knew how distressed *he* was..." (NIV, RV)
"...we saw *his* terror and anguish..." (TLB)
(Genesis 42:21)

"...let not my *soul* enter their council..." (NKJ)
"...O my *soul*, come not into their secrets..." (KJ)
"...*I* did not agree to sit in their counsels..." (L)
"...let *me* not enter into their council..." (NIV)
"...O *my soul*, stay away from them..." (TLB)
"...O *my soul*, come not into their counsel..." (RV)
(Genesis 49:6)

"...that *soul* shall be cut off from Israel..." (KJ)
"...that *person* shall be cut off from Israel..." (NKJ, RV)
"...that *person* shall perish from Israel..." (L)
"...*whoever* eats...must be cut off from Israel..." (NIV)
"...*anyone*...shall be excommunicated from Israel..." (TLB)
(Exodus 12:15)

"...even that *soul* shall be cut off..." (KJ)
"...that *person* shall be cut off..." (NKJ, RV)
"...that *person* shall perish..." (L)
"...*whoever* eats...must be cut off..." (NIV)
"...*anyone*...shall be excommunicated..." (TLB)
(Exodus 12:19)

"...a ransom for *his soul*..." (KJ, TLB)
"...a ransom for *himself*..." (NKJ, L, RV)
"...a ransom for *his life*..." (NIV)
(Exodus 30:12)

"...that *soul* shall be cut off..." (KJ, RV)
"...that *person* shall be cut off..." (NKJ)

"...that *soul* shall surely be cut off..." (L)
"...*whoever*...must be cut off..." (NIV)
"...*anyone*...shall be killed..." (TLB)
(Exodus 31:14)

"...if *a soul* shall sin..." (KJ, RV)
"...if *anyone* sins..." (NKJ)
"...if *a person* shall sin..." (L)
"...if the anointed *priest* sins..." (NIV)
"...*anyone*...who breaks any of my commandments..." (TLB)
(Leviticus 4:2; 5:1)

"...if a *soul* touch any unclean thing..." (KJ)
"...if a *person* touches any unclean thing..." (NKJ)
"...if any *person* touches any unclean thing..." (L)
"...if a *person* touches anything..." (NIV)
"...*anyone* touching anything...unclean..." (TLB)
"...if *anyone* touches an unclean thing..." (RV)
(Leviticus 5:2)

"...if a *soul* swear..." (KJ)
"...if a *person* swears..." (NKJ)
"...if any *person* swears..." (L)
"...if a *person*...takes an oath..." (NIV)
"...if *anyone* makes a rash vow..." (TLB)
"...if *anyone* utters...a rash oath..." (RV)
(Leviticus 5:4)

"...if a *soul* commit a trespass..." (KJ)
"...if a *person* commits a trespass..." (NKJ)
"...if any *person* commits a trespass..." (L)
"...when a *person* commits a violation..." (NIV)
"...if *anyone* sins..." (TLB)
"...if *anyone* commits a breach of faith..." (RV)
(Leviticus 5:15)

"...if a *soul* sin..." (KJ)
"...if a *person* sins..." (NKJ, NIV)

"...if any *person* sins..." (L)
"...*anyone* who disobeys..." (TLB)
"...if *anyone* sins..." (RV)
(Leviticus 5:17; 6:2)

"...and the *soul* that eateth..." (KJ)
"...and the *person* who eats of it..." (NKJ, L)
"...and the *person* who eats any of it..." (NIV)
"... and the *priest* who eats it..." (TLB)
"...and *he* who eats it..." (RV)
(Leviticus 7:18)

"...that *soul* shall be cut off..." (KJ)
"...that *person* shall be cut off..." (NKJ, L, NIV, RV)
"...the *priest*...shall be cut off..." (TLB)
(Leviticus 7:20)

"...the *soul* that touch any unclean thing..." (KJ)
"...the *person* who touches any unclean thing..." (NKJ)
"...the *person* that shall touch any unclean thing..." (L)
"...if *anyone* touches anything unclean..." (NIV)
"...*anyone* who touches anything...unclean..." (TLB)
"...if *anyone* touches an unclean things..." (RV)
(Leviticus 7:21)

"...that *soul* that eateth it..." (KJ)
"...the *person* who eats it..." (NKJ)
"...the *person* that eats it..." (L)
"...*anyone* who eats the fat..." (NIV)
"...*anyone* who eats...shall be outlawed..." (TLB)
"...*every person* shall be cut off..." (RV)
(Leviticus 7:25)

"...whatsoever *soul* it be that eateth any manor of blood..." (KJ)
"...*whoever* eats any blood..." (NKJ, RV)
"...*whosoever* eats any manor of blood..." (L)
"...if *anyone* eats blood..." (NIV)

"...*anyone* who does (eat blood)..." (TLB)
(Leviticus 7:27)

"...that *soul* shall be cut off..." (KJ)
"...that *person* shall be cut off..." (NKJ, RV)
"...the *person* that eats it shall be cut off..." (L)
"...that *person* must be cut off..." (NIV)
"...*anyone*...shall be excommunicated..." (TLB)
(Leviticus 7:27)

"...that *soul* that eateth blood..." (KJ)
"...that *person* who eats blood..." (NKJ, L, NIV)
"...*anyone*...who eats blood..."(TLB)
"...any *man*...or any *stranger*...who eats blood..." (RV)
(Leviticus 17:10)

"...to make an atonement for your *souls*..." (KJ, NKJ, TLB, RV)
"...to make an atonement for *yourselves*..." (L, NIV)
(Leviticus 17:11)

"...*no soul* of you shall eat blood..." (KJ)
"...*no one* among you shall eat blood..." (NKJ)
"...*no person* among you shall eat blood..." (L)
"...*none of you* shall eat blood..." (NIV)
"...*none of you* may eat blood..." (TLB)
"...*no person* among you shall eat blood..." (RV)
(Leviticus 17:12)

"...and every *soul* that eateth..." (KJ)
"...and every *person* who eats..." (NKJ, L)
"...*anyone*...who eats..." (NIV)
"...and *everyone* who eats..." (TLB)
"...and every *person* that eats..." (RV)
(Leviticus 17:15)

"...and *the soul* that turneth after..." (KJ)
"...and *the person* who turns to..." (NKJ)
"...and *the person* who goes after..." (L)

"...*the person* who turns..." (NIV)
"...*anyone* who consults..." (TLB)
"...if *a person* turns..." (RV)
(Leviticus 20:6)

"...I will set My face against that *soul*..." (KJ)
"...I will set My face against that *person*..." (NKJ, RV)
"...I will pour out My anger against that *person*..." (L)
"...I will cut *him* off..." (NIV)
"...I will cut that *person* off..." (TLB)
(Leviticus 20:6)

"...that *soul* shall be cut off..." (KJ)
"...that *person* shall be cut off..." (NKJ, L, RV)
"...that *person* must be cut off..." (NIV)
"...*he* shall be discharged..." (TLB)
(Leviticus 22:3)

"...the *soul* which hath touched..." (KJ)
"...the *person* who has touched..." (NKJ)
"...any *person* who touches..." (L, RV)
"...the *one* who touches..." (NIV)
"...any *priest* who touches..." (TLB)
(Leviticus 22:5-6)

"...if the priest buys any *soul*..." (KJ)
"...if the priest buys a *person*..." (NKJ)
"...if a priest buys any *person*..." (L)
"...if a priest buys a *slave*..." (NIV, TLB, RV)
(Leviticus 22:11)

"...for whosoever *soul* it be that shall not be afflicted..." (KJ)
"...for any *person* who is not afflicted in *soul*..." (NKJ)
"...for whatever *person* it be who does not humble *himself*..." (L)
"...*anyone* who does not deny *himself*..." (NIV)
"...*anyone* who does not spend the day in repentance..." (TLB)
"...*whoever* is not afflicted..." (RV)
(Leviticus 23:29)

"...whatsoever *soul* it be that doeth any work..." (KJ)
"...and any *person* who does any work..." (NKJ)
"...and whatever *person* it be who does any work..." (L)
"...*anyone* who does any work on that day..." (NIV, TLB)
"...*whoever* does any work..." (RV)
(Leviticus 23:30)

"...and the same *soul* will I destroy..." (KJ)
"...that *person* I will destroy..." (NKJ)
"...the same *person* will I destroy..." (L, RV)
"...I will destroy *anyone*..." (NIV)
"...and I will put to death *anyone*..." (TLB)
(Leviticus 23:30)

"...and My *soul* shall not abhor you..." (KJ, NKJ, L, RV)
"...and *I* will not abhor you..." (NIV)
"...*I*...will not despise you..." (TLB)
(Leviticus 26:11)

"...if your *soul* abhor my judgments..." (KJ)
"...if *you* despise my statutes..." (NKJ)
"...if *you* despise my laws..." (L)
"...if *you* reject my decrees..." (NIV)
"...but (*you*) reject my laws..." (TLB)
"...if *you* spurn my statutes..." (RV)
(Leviticus 26:15)

"...and *My soul* shall abhor you..." (KJ, NKJ, L, RV)
"...and *I* will abhor you..." (NIV, TLB)
(Leviticus 26:30)

"...because their *souls* abhorred My statutes..." (KJ, NKJ, L, RV)
"...because *they* have abhorred My judgments..."(NIV)
"...*(they)* shall accept their punishment for rejecting my laws..." (TLB)
(Leviticus 26:43)

"...even the same *soul*..." (KJ)
"...that same *person*..." (NKJ)

"...that *person*..." (L, RV)
"...that *man*..." (NIV)
"...*anyone*...shall be..." (TLB)
(Numbers 9:13)

"...our *soul* is dried away..." (KJ)
"...our *whole being* is dried up..." (NKJ)
"...our *soul* is dried up..." (L)
"...*we* have lost our appetite..." (NIV)
"...our *strength* is gone..." (TLB)
"...our *strength* is dried up..." (RV)
(Numbers 11:6)

"...if any *soul* sin..." (KJ)
"...if a *person* sins..." (NKJ, L)
"...if just one *person* sins..." (NIV)
"...a single *individual*..." (TLB)
"...if one *person*..." (RV)
(Numbers 15:27)

"...atonement for *the soul*..." (KJ)
"...atonement for *the person*..." (NKJ, L, RV)
"...atonement...for *the one* who erred..." (NIV)
"...atonement for *him*..." (TLB)
(Numbers 15:28)

"...the *soul* that doeth..." (KJ)
"...the *person*..." (NKJ, RV)
"...the *person* who..." (L)
"...*anyone* who..." (NIV, TLB)
(Numbers 15:30)

"...*that soul* shall be cut off..." (KJ)
"...*he* shall be cut off..." (NKJ)
"...*that person* shall be cut off..." (L)
"...*that person* must be cut off..." (NIV)
"...*anyone*...shall be cut off..." (TLB, RV)
(Numbers 15:30)

"...that *soul* shall utterly be cut off..." (KJ)
"...that *person* shall be completely cut off..." (NKJ)
"...that *person* shall utterly be cut off..." (L, RV)
"...that *person* must surely be cut off..." (NIV)
"...*he* must be executed..." (TLB)
(Numbers 15:31)

"...that *soul* shall be cut off..." (KJ)
"...that *person* shall be cut off..." (NKJ, L, RV)
"...that *person* must be cut off..." (NIV)
"...that *person* must be excommunicated..." (TLB)
(Numbers 19:13)

"...that *soul* shall be cut off..." (KJ, L)
"...that *person* shall be cut off..." (NKJ, RV)
"...*he* must be cut off..." (NIV)
"...that *person* must be excommunicated..." (TLB)
(Numbers 19:20)

"...and the *soul* that toucheth it..." (KJ)
"...and the *person* who touches it..." (NKJ, L)
"...and *anyone* who touches it..." (NIV)
"...the unclean *person* touches..." (RV)
"...the defiled *person* touches..." (TLB)
(Numbers 19:22)

"...and the *soul* of the people..." (KJ, NKJ)
"...the *people*..." (L, TLB, RV)
"...but the *people*..." (NIV)
(Numbers 21:4)

"...*our soul* loatheth this light bread..." (KJ)
"...*our soul* loaths this worthless bread..." (NKJ)
"...*our soul* is weary with this inferior bread..." (L)
"...*we* detest this miserable food..." (NIV)
"...*we* hate this insipid manna..." (TLB)
"...*we* loath this worthless food..." (RV)
(Numbers 21:5)

"...an oath to bind *his soul* with a bond..." (KJ)
"...swears an oath to bind *himself*..." (NKJ, L)
"...takes an oath to obligate *himself*..." (NIV)
"...*anyone...a promise* to the Lord..." (TLB)
"...a *man vows* to the Lord..." (RV)
(Numbers 30:2)

"...wherewith she hath bound her *soul*..." (KJ)
"...by which she bound *herself*..." (NKJ, L, RV)
"...by which she obligated *herself*..." (NIV)
"...*she made a vow...her vow* shall stand..." (TLB, RV)
(Numbers 30:4) (twice in this scripture)

"...wherewith she hath bound *her soul*..." (KJ)
"...by which she bound *herself*..." (NKJ, L, RV)
"...by which she obligated *herself*..." (NIV)
"...*her* promise..." (TLB)
(Numbers 30:5)

"...wherewith she bound *her soul*..." (KJ)
"...by which she bound *herself*..." (NKJ, L, RV)
"...by which she obligates *herself*..." (NIV)
"... *if she* takes a vow..." (TLB)
(Numbers 30:6)

"...wherewith she bound *her soul*..." (KJ)
"...by which she bound *herself*..." (NKJ, L)
"...by which she obligated *herself*..." (NIV)
"...*her* vows and pledges shall stand..." (TLB, RV)
(Numbers 30:7)

"...wherewith she bound *her soul*..." (KJ)
"...by which she bound *herself*..." (NKJ, L)
"...by which she obligates *herself*..." (NIV)
"...*her* vow of foolish pledge..." (TLB)
"...*her* vow which was on *her*..." (RV)
(Numbers 30:8)

"...or bound *her soul*..." (KJ)
"...or bound *herself*..." (NKJ, L, RV)
"...or obligates *herself*..." (NIV)
"...*she* makes the vow..." (TLB)
"...by which she bound *herself*..." (RV)
(Numbers 30:10)

"...wherewith she bound *her soul*..." (KJ)
"...by which she bound *herself*..." (NKJ)
"...bound *herself* with an oath..." (L)
"...by which she obligated *herself*..." (NIV)
"...(*her*) vow stands..." (TLB)
"...all *her* vows shall stand..." (RV)
(Numbers 30:11)

"...the bond of her *soul*..." (KJ)
"...the agreement binding *her*..." (NKJ)
"...by which she bound *herself*..." (L)
"...*her* vow..." (TLB, RV)
(Numbers 30:12)

"...every binding oath to afflict the *soul*..." (KJ, NKJ, L)
"...any vow *she* makes..." (NIV)
"...*her* vow..." (TLB)
"...any binding vow or oath to afflict *herself*..." (RV)
(Numbers 30:13)

"...one *soul* of five hundred..." (KJ)
"...*one* of every five hundred..." (NKJ, RV)
"...one *person* of every five hundred..." (L)
"...*one* out of every five hundred..." (NIV, TLB)
(Numbers 31:28)

"...and keep *thy soul* diligently..." (KJ, L, RV)
"...and diligently keep *yourself*..." (NKJ)
"...and watch *yourselves* closely..." (NIV)
"...*(you)* watch out. Be very careful..." (TLB)
(Deuteronomy 4:9)

"…in your heart and in your *soul…*" (KJ, NKJ, L, RV)
"…in your hearts and *minds…*" (NIV)
"…in *mind…*" (TLB)
(Deuteronomy 11:18)

"…whatsoever thy *soul* lusteth after…" (KJ)
"…whatever your *heart* desires…" (NKJ)
"…whatever your *soul* may desire…" (L)
"…as much…as *you* want…" (NIV)
"…as much...as *you* wish…" (TLB)
"…as much as *you* desire…" (RV)
(Deuteronomy 12:15)

"…because thy *soul* longeth…" (KJ)
"…because *you* long to…" (NKJ)
"…because your *soul* longs…" (L)
"…*you* crave…and say '*I* would like some…'" (NIV)
(Deuteronomy 12:20)

"…whatsoever thy *soul* lusteth after…" (KJ)
"…as your *heart* desires…" (NKJ)
"…whatever your *soul* may desire…" (L)
"…as much as *you* want…" (NIV)
"…as you say, '*I* will eat…'" (RV)
(Deuteronomy 12:20)

"…whatsoever thy *soul* lusteth after…" (KJ)
"…as much as your *heart* desires…" (NKJ)
"…whatever your *soul* may desire…" (L)
"…as much of them as *you* want…" (NIV)
"…as much as *you* desire…" (RV)
(Deuteronomy 12:21)

"…which friend who is *thine own soul…*" (KJ, L)
"…friend who is as *your own soul…*" (NKJ, RV)
"…your *closest friend…*" (NIV, TLB)
(Deuteronomy 13:6)

"...whatsoever thy *soul* lusteth after..." (KJ)
"...whatever your *heart* desires..." (NKJ)
"...whatever *you* desire..." (L, RV)
"...whatever *you* like..." (NIV)
(Deuteronomy 14:26)

"...whatsoever thy *soul* desireth..." (KJ)
"...whatever your *heart* desires..." (NKJ)
"...whatever *you* may desire..." (L)
"...anything *you* wish..." (NIV)
(Deuteronomy 14:26)

"...and *His soul* was grieved..." (KJ)
"...and *His soul* could no longer endure..." (NKJ)
"...the *soul of Israel* was grieved..." (L)
"...and *He* could bear Israel's misery no longer..." (NIV)
"...and *He* was grieved..." (TLB)
"...and *He* became indignant..." (RV)
(Judges 10:16)

"...*his soul* was vexed..." (KJ, NKJ, L, RV)
"...*he* was tired to death..." (NIV)
"...*he* couldn't stand it..." (TLB)
(Judges 16:16)

"...as *thy soul* liveth..." (KJ)
"...as *your soul* lives..." (NKJ, L)
"...as surely as *you* live..." (NIV)
"...as *you* live..." (RV)
(1 Samuel 1:26)

"...as *thy soul* liveth..." (KJ)
"...as *your soul* lives..." (NKJ, L, RV)
"...as surely as *you* live..." (NIV)
(1 Samuel 17:55)

"...the *soul* of Jonothan..." (KJ, NKJ, L, RV)

"...*one in spirit* with Jonothan..." (NIV)
(1 Samuel 18:1)

"...the *soul* of David..." (KJ, NKJ, L, RV)
"...loved *him* as *himself*..." (NIV)
(1 Samuel 18:1)

"...as his *own soul*..." (KJ, NKJ, L, RV)
"...loved *him as himself*..." (NIV)
(1 Samuel 18:1)

"...loved him as *his own soul*..." (KJ, NKJ, L, RV)
"...loved him as *himself*..." (NIV)
"...a bond of love between *them*..." (TLB)
(1 Samuel 18:3)

"...as *thy soul* lives..." (KJ)
"...as *your soul* lives..." (NKJ)
"...as *the Lord* lives..." (L, RV)
"...and as *you* live..." (NIV, RV)
"...*I* swear..." (TLB)
(1 Samuel 20:3)

"...whosoever *thy soul* desireth..." (KJ)
"...whatever *you yourself* desire..." (NKJ)
"...whatever *you* desire..." (L)
"...whatever *you* want me to do..." (NIV)
"...what can I do (for *you*)..." (TLB)
"...whatever *you* say, I will do..." (RV)
(1 Samuel 20:4)

"...he loved him as he loved *his own soul*..." (KJ, NKJ, L, RV)
"...he loved him as he loved *himself*..." (NIV)
"...as much as he loved *himself*..." (TLB)
(1 Samuel 20:17)

"...come...according to all the *desire of Thy soul*..." (KJ, NKJ, L)
"...come...according to all *your heart's desire*..." (RV)

"...come...whenever it pleases *You*..." (NIV)
"...(*you*) come on down..." (TLB)
(1 Samuel 23:20)

"...yet thou huntest *my soul* to take it..." (KJ)
"...yet you hunt *my life* to take it..." (NKJ, RV)
"...yet you hunt *me* to take my life..." (L)
"...you are hunting me down to take *my life*..." (NIV)
"...you have been hunting for *my life*..." (TLB)
(1 Samuel 24:11)

"...as the Lord liveth and as *thy soul* liveth..." (KJ)
"...as the Lord lives and as *your soul* lives..." (NKJ, L, RV)
"...as the Lord lives and as *you* live..." (NIV)
"...by the life of God and my *your own life*, too..." (TLB)
(1 Samuel 25:26)

"...and to seek *thy soul*..." (KJ)
"...and seek *your life*..." (NKJ, L, RV)
"...to take *your life*..." (NIV)
"...who seek *your life*..." (TLB)
(1 Samuel 25:29)

"...the *souls* of thine enemies..." (KJ)
"...the *lives* of your enemies..." (NKJ, L, NIV, TLB, RV)
(1 Samuel 25:29)

"...for *my soul* was precious..." (KJ)
"...for *my life* was precious..." (NKJ, L, RV)
"...you considered *my life* precious..." (NIV)
"...you saved *my life*..." (TLB)
(1 Samuel 26:21)

"...the *soul of all the people* was grieved..." (KJ, NKJ, L)
"...*each one* was bitter in spirit..." (NIV)
"...all the people were bitter in *soul*..." (RV)
"...in their bitter grief...*the men*..." (TLB)
(1 Samuel 30:6)

"…who has redeemed *my soul* out of all adversity…" (KJ)
"…who has redeemed *my life* from all adversity…" (NKJ)
"…who has saved *my life* out of every adversary…" (L)
"…who has delivered *me* out of all trouble…" (NIV)
(2 Samuel 4:9)

"…that are hated of David's *soul*…" (KJ, NKJ, L, RV)
"…who are David's *enemies*…" (NIV)
"…how *I* hate them…" (TLB)
(2 Samuel 5:8)

"…as *thy soul* liveth…" (KJ)
"…as *you* live…" (NKJ, L, NIV, RV)
"…*I* swear…" (TLB)
(2 Samuel 11:11)

"…the *soul of King David* longed to…" (KJ)
"…and *King David* longed…" (NKJ, L)
"…and *the spirit of the king* longed…" (NIV, RV)
"…*King David*…longed, day after day…" (TLB)
(2 Samuel 13:39)

"…as *thy soul* liveth…" (KJ)
"…as *you* live…" (NKJ)
"…as *your soul* lives…" (L)
"…as surely as *you* live…" (NIV, RV)
(2 Samuel 14:19)

"…that hath redeemed *my soul*…" (KJ)
"…that has redeemed *my life* from every distress…" (NKJ)
"…Who has saved *my soul* out of all distress…" (L)
"…Who has delivered *me* out of every trouble…" (NIV)
"…Who has rescued *me* from every danger…" (TLB)
(1 Kings 1:29)

"…according to all *thy soul* desireth…" (KJ, L)
"…all *your heart* desires…" (NKJ)

"...all that *your heart* desires..." (NIV)
"...all that *your soul* desires..." (RV)
"...and give *you* absolute power..." (TLB)
(1 Kings 11:37)

"...let this *child's soul* come into him again..." (KJ, NKJ, L, RV)
"...let this *boy's life* return to him..." (NIV)
"...let this *child's spirit* return to him..." (TLB)
(1 Kings 17:21)

"...and the *soul* of the child came into him again..." (KJ, RV)
"...and the *soul* of the child came back to him..." (NKJ)
"...and the *soul* of the boy returned to him..." (L)
"...and the boy's *life* returned to him..." (NIV)
"...and he became *alive* again..." (TLB)
(1 Kings 17:22)

"...and as *thy soul* liveth..." (KJ)
"...as *your soul* lives..." (NKJ, L)
"...and as *you* live..." (NIV)
"...*I* swear to you..." (L)
"...as *the Lord* lives..." (RV)
"...*I* swear to God..." (TLB)
"...as *you yourself* live..." (RV)
(2 Kings 2:2, 4, 6; 4:30)

"...*her soul* is vexed within her..." (KJ)
"...*her soul* is in deep distress..." (NKJ)
"...*her soul* is in bitter anguish..." (L)
"...*she* is in bitter distress..." (NIV, RV)
"...something is deeply troubling *her*..." (TLB)
(2 Kings 4:27)

"...*my soul* refuses to touch..." (KJ, NKJ)
"...*my soul* is weary of its troubles..." (L)
"...*I* refuse to touch it..." (NIV)
"...that are loathsome to *me*..." (RV)

"...*I* gag at the thought of eating it..." (TLB)
(Job 6:7)

"...*my soul* chooseth strangling and death rather than my life..." (KJ)
"...*my* soul chooses strangling and death rather than my body..." (NKJ)
"...*my life* out of destruction, and my bones out of death..." (L)
"...*I* prefer strangling and death..." (NIV)
"...*I* would rather die of strangulation..." (TLB)
(Job 7:15)

"...I would not know *my soul*..." (KJ, L)
"...I would not know *myself*..." (NKJ)
"...I have no concern for *myself*..." (NIV)
"...I despise what *I* am..."(TLB)
"...I loathe *my life*..." (RV)
(Job 9:21)

"...*my soul* is weary of my life..." (KJ, L)
"...*my soul* loathes my life..." (NKJ)
"...*I* loath my very life..." (NIV)
"...*I* am weary of living..." (TLB)
"...*I* loathe my life..." (RV)
(Job 10:1)

"...in whose hand is the *soul* of every living thing..." (KJ)
"...in whose hand is the *life* of every living thing..." (NKJ)
"...are the *souls* of every living thing..." (L)
"...in His hand is the *life* of every creature..." (NIV)
"...in His hand is the *life* of every living thing..." (RV)
"...the *soul* of every living thing is in the hand of God..." (TLB)
(Job 12:10)

"...and his *soul* within him shall mourn..." (KJ, L)
"...and his *soul* will mourn over it..." (NKJ)
"...*he*... mourns only for himself..." (NIV)
"...for *him* there is only sorrow and pain..." (TLB)

"...*he* mourns only for himself...(R)
(Job 14:22)

"...if *your soul* were in *my soul's* stead..." (KJ, NKJ)
"...I wish *you* were in *my* place..." (L)
"...if *you* were in *my* place..." (NIV, RV)
"...if *you* were I and *I* were you..." (TLB)
(Job 16:4)

"...how long will you vex *my soul...*" (KJ)
"...how long will you torment *my soul...*" (NKJ)
"...how long will you grieve *my soul...*" (L)
"...how long will you torment *me...*" (NIV, RV)
"...how long are you going to trouble *me...*" (TLB)
(Job 19:2)

"...what *his soul* desireth..." (KJ)
"...whatever *his soul* desires..." (NKJ)
"...what *his soul* desires..." (L)
"...what *he* desires..." (RV)
"...whatever *he* pleases..." (NIV)
"...whatever *he* wants to do..." (TLB)
(Job 23:13)

"...when God taketh away *his soul...*" (KJ)
"...if God takes away *his life...*" (NKJ)
"...when God takes away *his life...*" (L, NIV)
"...when God cuts him off and takes away his *life...*" (TLB, RV)
(Job 27:8)

"...they pursue *my soul...*" (KJ)
"...they pursue *my honor...*" (NKJ)
"...they have pursued *my paths...*" (L)
"...*my dignity* is driven away..." (NIV)
"...*my prosperity* has vanished..." (TLB)
"...*my honor* is pursued..." (RV)
(Job 30:15)

"...*my soul* is poured out..." (KJ, NKJ, RV)
"...*my soul* is weary..." (L)
"...*my life* ebbs away..." (NIV)
"...*my heart* is broken..." (TLB)
(Job 30:16)

"...by wishing a curse to *his soul*..." (KJ)
"...by asking a curse on *his soul*..." (NKJ)
"...nor has *my soul* wished for any of these things..." (L)
"...*I* have not allowed my mouth to sin by invoking a curse against *his life*..." (NIV, RV)
"...I have never cursed *anyone*..." (TLB)
(Job 31:30)

"...many there be who say of *my soul*..." (KJ, L)
"...Many are they who say of *me*..." (NKJ)
"...Many are saying of *me*..." (NIV, RV)
"...so many say that God will never help *me*..."(TLB)
(Psalms 3:2)

"...return Oh Lord, deliver *my soul*..." (KJ, L)
"...return Oh Lord, deliver *me*..." (NKJ)
"...turn Oh Lord, and deliver *me*..." (NIV)
"...turn Oh Lord and save *my life*..." (RV)
"...come Oh Lord, and make *me* well..." (TLB)
(Psalms 6:4)

"...lest he tear *my soul* like a lion..." (KJ)
"...lest they tear *me* like a lion..." (NKJ)
"...lest *my soul* be torn like a lion..." (L)
"...or they will tear *me* like a lion..." (NIV)
"...don't let them pounce upon *me* like a lion would..." (TLB)
"...lest like a lion they rend *me*..." (RV)
(Psalms 7:2)

"...let the enemy persecute *my soul*..." (KJ)
"...let the enemy pursue *me* and overtake *me*..." (NKJ, L, NIV)

"...let my enemies destroy *me*..." (TLB)
(Psalms 7:5)

"...how say ye to *my soul*..." (KJ, NKJ)
"...how say you to *me*..." (L)
"...how can you say to *me*..." (NIV, RV)
"...how dare you tell *me*..." (TLB)
(Psalms 11:1)

"...how long shall I take counsel in *my soul*..." (KJ, NKJ)
"...how long shall I keep sorrow in *my soul*..." (L)
"...how long must I wrestle with *my thoughts*..." (NIV)
"...how long shall I keep hiding daily anguish in *my heart*..." (TLB)
"...how long must I bear pain in *my soul*..." (RV)
(Psalms 13:2)

"...Oh *my soul*, though hast said unto the Lord..." (KJ, NKJ)
"...*I* have said unto the Lord..." (L)
"...*I* said to the Lord..." (NIV, RV)
"...*I* said to Him..." (TLB)
(Psalms 16:2)

"...for thou wilt not leave *my soul* in hell..."(KJ)
"...for you will not leave *my soul* to shoel..." (NKJ)
"...for thou hast not left *my soul* in shoel..." (L)
"...because you will not abandon *me* to the grave..." (NIV)
"...for though dost not give *me* up to shoel..." (RV)
(Psalms 16:10)

"...deliver *my soul* from the wicked..." (KJ, L)
"...deliver *my life* from the wicked..." (NKJ, RV)
"...rescue *me* from the wicked..." (NIV)
"...save *me* from these men of the world..." (TLB)
(Psalms 17:13)

"...deliver *my soul* from the sword..." (KJ, L, RV)
"...deliver *me* from the sword..." (NKJ)

"...deliver *my life* from the sword..." (NIV)
"...rescue *me* from death..." (TLB)
(Psalms 22:20)

"...none can keep alive *his own soul*..." (KJ)
"...even he who cannot keep *himself* alive..." (NKJ)
"...*my soul* is alive to Him..." (L)
"...those who cannot keep *themselves* alive..." (NIV)
"...he who cannot keep *himself* alive..." (RV)
(Psalms 22:29)

"...*his soul* shall dwell at ease..." (KJ)
"...*he himself* shall dwell in prosperity..." (NKJ, RV)
"...*his soul* shall abide with grace..." (L)
"...*he* will spend his days in prosperity..." (NIV)
"...*he* shall live within God's circle of blessings..." (TLB)
(Psalms 25:13)

"...keep *my soul*..." (KJ, NKJ, L)
"...guard *my life*..." (NIV, RV)
"...save *me*..." (TLB)
(Psalms 25:20)

"...gather not *my soul* with sinners...." (KJ)
"...do not gather *my soul* with sinners..." (NKJ)
"...destroy *me* not with sinners..." (L)
"...do not take away *my soul* with sinners..." (NIV)
"...don't treat *me* as a common sinner..." (TLB)
"...sweep *me* not away with sinners..." (RV)
(Psalms 26:9)

"...Thou hast brought up *my soul* from the grave..." (KJ)
"...You brought *my soul* up from the grave..." (NKJ
"...Thou has brought up *my soul* from Shoel..." (L, RV)
"...You brought *me* up from the grave..." (NIV)
"...You brought *me* back from the brink of the grave..." (TLB)
(Psalms 30:3)

"…to deliver *their soul* from death…" (KJ, NKJ, L, RV)
"…to keep *them* alive in famine…" (NIV)
"…He will keep *them* from death…" (TLB)
(Psalms 33:19)

"…*our soul* waiteth for the Lord…" (KJ)
"…*our soul* waits for the Lord…" (NKJ, L, RV)
"…*we* wait in hope for the Lord…" (NIV)
"…*we* can depend on the Lord…" (TLB)
(Psalms 33:20)

"…the Lord redeemeth *the soul* of his servant…" (KJ)
"…the Lord redeems *the soul* of his servants…" (NKJ, L)
"…the Lord redeems *his servants…*" (NIV)
"…he will redeem *them…*" (TLB)
"…the Lord redeems *the life* of his servants…" (RV)
(Psalms 34:22)

"…say unto *my soul…*" (KJ, NKJ, L, NIV, RV)
"…let *me* hear you say…" (TLB)
(Psalms 35:3)

"…that seek after *my soul…*" (KJ, L)
"…who seek after *my life…*" (NKJ, RV)
"…who plot *my ruin…*" (NIV)
"…who are trying to kill *me…*" (TLB)
(Psalms 35:4)

"…they have digged for *my soul…*" (KJ)
"…they have dug…for *my life…*" (NKJ)
"…they have dug pits for *me…*" (L)
"…dug a pit for *me…*" (NIV)
"…they laid a trap for *me…*" (TLB)
"…they hid their net for *me…*" (RV)
(Psalms 35:7)

"…to the spoiling of *my soul…*" (KJ)
"…to the sorrow of *my soul…*" (NKJ)

"...they destroyed *my reputation*..." (L)
"...and leave *my soul* forlorn..." (NIV, RV)
"...*I* am sinking down to death..." (TLB)
(Psalms 35:12)

"...I humbled *my soul*..." (KJ, L)
"...I humbled *myself*..." (NKJ)
"...and humbled *myself*..." (NIV)
"...*I* prayed for them with utmost earnestness." (TLB)
"...I afflicted *myself*..." (RV)
(Psalms 35:13)

"...rescue *my soul*..." (KJ, L)
"...rescue *me*..." (NKJ)
"...rescue *my life*..." (NIV)
(Psalms 35:17)

"...that seek after *my soul* to destroy it..." (KJ, L)
"...who seek to destroy *my life*..." (NKJ)
"...who seek to take *my life*..." (NIV)
"...all those who seek to destroy *me*..." (TLB)
"...who seek to snatch away *my life*..." (RV)
(Psalms 40:14)

"...heal *my soul*..." (KJ, L, NKJ)
"...heal *me*..." (NIV, TLB, RV)
(Psalms 41:4)

"...for *our soul* is bowed down to the dust..." (KJ, NKJ, RV)
"...for *our soul* is humbled down to the dust..." (L)
"...*We* are brought down to the dust..." (NIV)
"...*we* lie face downward..." (TLB)
(Psalms 44:25)

"...for the redemption of their *souls* is precious..." (KJ, L, NKJ)
"...the ransom for a *life* is costly..." (NIV)
"...a *soul* is far too precious to be ransomed..." (TLB)

"...for the ransom of his *life*..." (RV)
(Psalms 49:8)

"...but God will redeem *my soul*..." (KJ, L, NKJ, TLB)
"...but God will ransom *my soul*..." (RV)
"...but God will redeem *my life*..." (NIV)
(Psalms 49:15)

"...while he lived, he blessed *his soul*..." (KJ)
"...while he lives, he blesses *himself*..." (NKJ)
"...while he lived, *he* lived comfortably..." (L)
"...while he lived, he counted *himself* blessed..."(NIV)
"...man calls *himself* happy all through his life..." (TLB)
"...while he lives, he calls *himself* happy..." (RV)
(Psalms 49:18)

"...and oppressors seek after *my soul*..." (KJ)
"...and oppressors have sought after *my life*..." (NKJ)
"...strangers are attacking *me*..." (NIV)
"...violent men have risen against *me*..." (TLB)
"...insolent men have risen against *me*..." (RV)
(Psalms 54:3)

"...the Lord is with them that uphold *my soul*..." (KJ)
"...the Lord is with those who uphold *my life*..."(NKJ)
"...the Lord sustains *my soul*..." (L)
"...the Lord is the one who sustains *me*..." (NIV)
"...God is *my* helper..." (TLB)
"...God is the upholder of *my life*..." (RV)
(Psalms 54:4)

"...He hath delivered *my soul* in peace..." (KJ)
"...He hath redeemed *my soul*..." (NKJ)
"...He ransoms *me* unharmed..." (NIV)
"...He will rescue *me*..." (TLB)
"...He will deliver *my soul*..." (RV)
(Psalms 55:18)

"...when they wait for *my soul*..." (KJ)
"...they lie in wait for *my life*..." (NKJ)
"...they wish for *my death*..."(L)
"...eager to take *my life*..." (NIV)
"...waiting to kill *me*..." (TLB)
"...they watch *my* steps..." (RV)
(Psalms 56:6)

"...for thou hast delivered *my soul*..." (KJ, L, NKJ, RV)
"...for you have delivered *me*..." (NIV)
"...you have saved *me* from death..." (TLB)
(Psalms 56:13)

"...*my soul* is among lions..." (KJ, NKJ)
"...*I* am among lions..." (NIV)
"...*I* am surrounded by fierce lions..." (TLB)
"...*I* lie in the midst of lions..." (RV)
(Psalms 57:4)

"...they have digged a pit for *me*..." (KJ)
"...they have dug a pit before *me*..." (NKJ)
"...they dug a pit in *my* path..." (NIV)
"...they have digged a pit for *my soul*..." (L)
"...they have prepared a net for *my* steps..." (RV)
"...(they) have set a trap for *me*..." (TLB)
(Psalms 57:6)

"...for they lie in wait for my *soul*..." (KJ)
"...for they lie in wait for my *life*..." (NKJ, RV)
"...lo, they lie in wait for my *soul*..." (L)
"...they lie in wait for *me*..." (NIV)
"...they lurk in ambush for my *life*..." (TLB)
(Psalms 59:3)

"...they seek *my soul*..." (KJ, L)
"...they seek *my life*..." (NKJ, NIV)
"...those plotting to destroy *me*..." (TLB)

"...those who seek to destroy *my life...*" (RV)
(Psalms 63:9)

"...who hold *our soul* in life..." (KJ, L)
"...who keeps *our soul* among the living..." (NKJ)
"...He has preserved *our lives...*" (NIV)
"...who holds *our lives* in His hand..." (TLB)
"...who has kept us among *the living...*" (RV)
(Psalms 66:9)

"...I will declare what He has done for *my soul...*" (KJ, L, NKJ)
"...let me tell you what He had done for *me...*" (NIV)
"...I will tell you what he did for *me...*" (TLB, RV)
(Psalms 66:16)

"...for the waters are come into *my soul...*" (KJ)
"...where the floods overflow *me...*" (L)
"...for the waters have come up to *my* neck..." (NKJ, NIV, RV)
"...the waters rise around *me...*" (TLB)
(Psalms 69:1)

"...draw near unto *my soul* and redeem *it...*" (KJ, L, NKJ)
"...draw near to *me,* redeem *me...*" (RV)
"...come near and rescue *me*, redeem *me...*" (NIV)
"...come Lord and rescue *me...*" (TLB)
(Psalms 69:18)

"...that seek after *my soul...*" (KJ, L)
"...that seek *my life...*" (NKJ)
"...those who seek *my life...*" (NIV, RV)
"...(those) who are after *my life...*" (TLB)
(Psalms 70:2)

"...they that lie in wait for *my soul...*" (KJ, L)
"...those who lie in wait for *my life...*" (NKJ)
"...those who wait to kill *me...*" (NIV)
(Psalms 71:10)

"…that are adversaries to *my soul*…" (KJ)
"…those who are adversaries of *my life*…" (NKJ)
"…who envy *my soul*…" (L)
"…those who want to harm *me*…" (NIV)
"…those who watch for *my life*…" (RV)
"…my enemies are whispering (about *me*)…" (TLB)
(Psalms 71:13)

"…my *soul* which thou hast redeemed…" (KJ, L, NKJ, RV)
"…*I*, whom you have redeemed…" (NIV)
"…for redeeming *me*…" (TLB)
(Psalms 71:23)

"…He shall redeem *their souls*…" (KJ, L, LV)
"…He will redeem *their life*…" (NKJ)
"…He will rescue *them*…" (NIV)
"…He redeems *their life*…" (RV)
"…He will save *them*…" (TLB)
(Psalms 72:14)

"…the *soul* of thy turtle dove…" (KJ, RV)
"…the *life* of your turtle dove…" (NKJ)
"…the *soul* that confesses to thee..." (L)
"…the *life* of your dove…" (NIV)
"…save *me*, protect your turtle dove…" (TLB)
(Psalms 74:19)

"…He spared not *their souls* from death…" (KJ, L)
"…He did not spare *their souls* from death…" (NKJ)
"…He did not spare *them* from death…" (NIV)
"…He did not spare the *Egyptians* lives…" (TLB)
(Psalms 78:50)

"…preserve *my soul*…" (KJ, L)
"…preserve *my life*…" (NKJ, RV)
"…Guard *my life*…" (NIV)
"…protect *me* from death…" (TLB)
(Psalms 86:2)

"...rejoice the *soul of Thy servant...*" (KJ, L, NKJ)
"...gladden the *soul of Thy servant...*" (RV)
"...give *me* happiness..." (TLB)
(Psalms 86:4)

"...Thou hast delivered *my soul...*" (KJ, L, NKJ, RV)
"...You have delivered *me...*" (NIV)
"...You have rescued *me...*" (TLB)
(Psalms 86:13)

"...violent men has sought after *my soul...*" (KJ, L)
"...violent men have sought *my life...*" (NKJ)
"...the arrogant are attacking *me...*" (NIV)
"...violent, Godless men are trying to kill *me...*" (TLB)
"...a band of ruthless men seek *my life...*" (RV)
(Psalms 86:14)

"...why casteth Thou off *my soul...*" (NKJ)
"...forsake not *my soul...*" (L)
"...why...do You reject *me...*" (NIV)
"...why have You thrown *my life* away..." (TLB)
"...why hast Thou swept over *me...*" (RV)
(Psalms 88:14)

"...deliver *his soul...*" (KJ, L, RV)
"...can he deliver *his life...*" (NKJ)
"...can...he save *himself...*" (NIV)
"...can rescue *his life...*" (TLB)
(Psalms 89:48)

"...*my soul* had almost dwelt in silence..." (KJ, NKJ, RV)
"...*my soul* would soon have been in trouble..." (L)
"...*I* would soon have dwelt in the silence of death..." (NIV)
"...*I* would have died..." (TLB)
(Psalms 94:17)

"...they gather themselves together against the *soul...*" (KJ)

"...they gather together against the *life* of the righteous..."(NKJ)
"...they lay snares to trap the *soul*..." (L)
"...they band together against the *righteous*..." (NIV)
"...they joined forces against *the life*..." (RV)
"...those who condemn the *innocent* to death..." (TLB)
(Psalms 94:21)

"...hungry and thirsty, *their soul* fainted in them..." (KJ, L, NKJ)
"...hungry and thirsty and *their lives* ebbed away..." (NIV)
"...hungry and thirsty, *their souls* became faint..." (TLB, RV)
(Psalms 107:5)

"...for He satisfied *the longing soul*...
and fills *the hungry soul* with goodness..."(KJ, L, NKJ)
"...for He satisfies *the thirsty*...
and fills *the hungry* with good things..." (NIV)
"...for He satisfies the *thirsty soul*...
and fill the hungry with good..." (TLB)
"...for He satisfies *him* who is thirsty,
and the hungry He fill with good things..." (RV)
(Psalms 107:9)

"...*their souls* abhorred all manner of food..." (KJ, L, NKJ)
"...*they* loathed all food..." (NIV, RV)
"...*their* appetites were gone..." (TLB)
(Psalms 107:18)

"...their *soul* is melted because of trouble..." (KJ, NKJ)
"...their *soul* is troubled within them..." (L)
"...*their* courage melted away..." (NIV)
"...the *sailors* cringe in terror..." (TLB)
"...*they* went down to the depths..." (RV)
(Psalms 107:26)

"...and of them that speak evil against *my soul*..." (KJ)
"...and to those who speak evil against *my person*..." (NKJ)
"...and if those who speak evil against *me*..." (L)

"...to those who speak evil of *me*..." (NIV)
(Psalms 109:20)

"...to save him from those who condemn *his soul*..." (KJ)
"...to save him from those who condemn *him*..." (NKJ)
"...to save *his soul* from judgment..." (L)
"...to save *his life* from those who condemn him..." (NIV)
(Psalms 109:31)

"...deliver *my soul*..." (KJ, L, NKJ)
"...save *me*..." (NIV)
(Psalms 116:4)

"...*my soul* cleaveth unto the dust..." (KJ, L, NKJ)
"...*I* am laid low in the dust..." (NIV)
(Psalms 119:25)

"...*my soul* is continually in my hand..." (KJ)
"...my *life* is continually in my hand..." (NKJ)
"...*my soul* is continually in thy hands..." (L)
"...I constantly take *my life* in my hands..."(NIV)
(Psalms 119:109)

"...thy testimonies are wonderful, therefore doth
my soul keep them..." (KJ, L, NKJ)
"...your statutes are wonderful, therefore *I* obey them..." (NIV)
(Psalms 119:129)

"...*my soul* hath kept Thy testimonies..." (KJ, L, NKJ)
"...*I* obey your statutes..." (NIV)
"...*I* have looked for your commandments..." (TLB)
"...*my soul* keeps Thy testimonies..." (RV)
(Psalms 119:167)

"...let *my soul* live..." (KJ, L, NKJ)
"...let *me* live..." (NIV, TLB, RV)
(Psalms 119:175)

"...deliver *my soul*, O Lord..." (KJ, L, NKJ)
"...save *me*, O Lord..." (NIV)
"...deliver *me*..." (TLB, RV)
(Psalms 120:2)

"...*my soul* has long dwelt..." (KJ, L, NKJ)
"...too long have *I* lived..." (NIV)
"...*my* troubles pile high..." (TLB)
"...too long have *I*..." (RV)
(Psalms 120:6)

"...He shall preserve *thy soul*..." (KJ)
"...the Lord shall preserve *you* from all evil..." (NKJ)
"...He will preserve *your soul*..." (L)
"...The Lord will keep *you* from all harm..." (NIV)
"...and preserve *your life*..." (TLB)
"...He will keep *your life*..." (RV)
(Psalms 121:7)

"...*our soul* is exceedingly filled with the scorning..." (KJ, NKJ)
"...*our soul* has enough of the scorn..." (L)
"...*we* have endured much ridicule..." (NIV)
"...*we* have had our fill..." (TLB)
"...too long *our souls* have been..." (RV)
(Psalms 123:4)

"...the stream had gone over *our soul*..." (KJ)
"...then the waters would have overwhelmed *us*..." (NKJ)
"...the stream would have gone over *us*..." (L)
"...the torrent would have swept over *us*..." (NIV)
"...*we* would have been drowned..." (TLB)
"...the flood would have swept *us* away..." (RV)
(Psalms 124:4)

"...the proud waters had gone over *our soul*..." (KJ)
"...the swollen waters would have gone over *our souls*..." (NKJ)
"...the great waters would have gone over *us*..." (L)
"...the raging waters would have swept *us* away..." (NIV)

"...the torrent would have gone over *us*..." (RV)
(Psalms 124:5)

"...*our soul* has escaped as a bird..." (KJ, NKJ, L)
"...*we* have escaped like a bird..." (NIV, RV)
"...*we* have escaped with our lives..." (TLB)
(Psalms 124:7)

"...*my soul* doth wait..." (KJ)
"...*my soul* waits..." (L, RV)
"...*I* wait for the Lord..." (NKJ, NIV)
"...*I* wait expectantly..." (TLB)
(Psalms 130:5)

"...*my soul* waits for the Lord..." (KJ, NKJ, NIV, RV)
"...*I* have waited for the Lord..." (L)
"...*I* long for Him..." (TLB)
(Psalms 130:6)

"...with strength in *my soul...* "(KJ)
"...and did increase the strength of *my soul*..." (NKJ, L)
"...You made *me* bold and stouthearted..." (NIV)
"...giving *me* the strength I need..." (TLB)
"...*my* strength of *soul* you did increase..." (RV)
(Psalms 138:3)

"...and *that, my soul* knowest..." (KJ, NKJ, L)
"...and *that I* know full well..." (NIV)
"...how well *I* know it..." (TLB)
"...Thou knowest *me* right well..." (RV)
(Psalms 139:14)

"...leave not *my soul* destitute..." (KJ)
"...do not leave *my soul* destitute..." (NKJ)
"...do not give *me* over to death..." (NIV)
"...don't let them slay *me*..." (TLB)

"...leave *me* not defenseless..." (RV)
(Psalms 141:8)

"...no man cared for *my soul*..." (KJ, L)
"...no one cares for *my soul*..." (NKJ)
"...no man cares for *my life*..." (NIV)
"...no man cares for *me*..." (RV)
"...no one cares a bit what happens to *me*..." (TLB)
(Psalms 142:4)

"...Bring *my soul* out of prison..." (KJ, NKJ, L)
"...Set *me* free from my prison..." (NIV)
"...bring *me* out of prison..." (TLB, RV)
(Psalms 142:7)

"...for the enemy has persecuted *my soul*..." (KJ,NKJ, L)
"...the enemy pursues *me*..." (NIV)
"...my enemy has pursued *me*..." (RV)
"...my enemies chased and caught *me*..." (TLB)
(Psalms 143:3)

"...bring *my soul* out of trouble..." (KJ, NKJ, L)
"...bring *me* out of trouble..." (NIV, TLB)
"...preserve *my life*..." (RV)
(Psalms 143:11)

"...destroy all those that afflict my *soul*..." (KJ, NKJ)
"...destroy all the enemies of my *soul*..." (L)
"...destroy all *my* foes..." (NIV)
"...cut off all *my* enemies..." (TLB)
"...destroy all *my* adversaries..." (RV)
(Psalms 143:12)

"...So shall they be life unto *thy soul*..." (KJ, NKJ, L)
"...they shall be life to *your soul*..." (RV)
"...they will be life for *you*..." (NIV)
"...they will fill *you*..." (TLB)
(Proverbs 3:22)

"...do not despise a thief if he steals to satisfy *his soul* when *he* is hungry..." (KJ)
"...do not despise a thief if *he* steals to satisfy *himself* when he is hungry..." (NKJ, RV)
"...he steals to satisfy *himself* when *he* is hungry..." (L)
"...do not despise a thief when *he* steals to satisfy *his* hunger..." (NIV)
"...excuses might even be found for a thief if *he* steals when *he* is starving..." (TLB)
(Proverbs 6:30)

"...he that doeth it destroyeth his own *soul*..." (KJ)
"...he that does so destroys his own *soul*..." (NKJ)
"...he destroys his own *soul*..." (L, TLB)
"...whoever does so, destroys *himself*..." (NIV, RV)
(Proverbs 6:32)

"...wrongeth *his own soul*..."(KJ)
"...wrongs *his own soul*..." (NKJ)
"...wrong *their own soul*..."(L)
"...harms *himself*..." (NIV)
"...has injured *himself*..." (TLB, RV)
(Proverbs 8:36)

"...the Lord will not suffer the *soul* of the righteous to famish..." (KJ,L)
"... the Lord will not allow the righteous *soul* to famish..." (NKJ)
"...the Lord does not let *the righteous* to go hungry..." (NIV, RV)
"...the Lord will not let the good *man* starve to death..." (TLB)
(Proverbs 10:3)

"...The merciful man doeth good to *his own soul*... (KJ, NKJ)
"...a pious man does good to *his soul*..." (L)
"...a kind man benefits *himself*..." (NIV, RV)
"...*your own soul* is nourished when you are kind..." (TLB)
(Proverbs 11:17)

"...the liberal *soul* shall be made fat..." (KJ)

"...the generous *soul* will be made rich..." (NKJ)
"...the liberal *soul* shall be enriched..." (L)
"...a liberal *man* shall be enriched..." (RV)
"...a generous *man* will prosper..." (NIV)
"...the liberal *man* will be rich..." (TLB)
(Proverbs 11:25)

"...but the *soul* of the transgressors shall eat violence..." (KJ)
"...but the *soul* of the unfaithful feeds on violence..." (NKJ)
"...but the *souls* of the wicked shall perish..." (L)
"...but the *unfaithful* have a craving for violence..." (NIV)
"...but the *desire* of the treacherous is for violence..." (RV)
"...the *evil minded* only wants to fight..." (TLB)
(Proverbs 13:2)

"...the *soul* of the sluggard desireth but hath nothing; but the *soul* of the diligent shall be made fat..." (KJ)
"...the *soul* of a lazy man desires but has nothing; but the *soul* of the diligent shall be made rich..." (NKJ)
"...a *sluggard* is always craving; but the *soul* of the diligent shall be enriched..." (L)
"...the *sluggard* craves and get nothing, but the desires of the *diligent* are full satisfied..." (NIV)
"...the *soul* of the sluggard craves and get nothing, while the *soul* of the diligent is richly supplied..." (RV)
"...lazy *people* want much but get little, while the *diligent* are prospering..." (TLB)
(Proverbs 13:4)

"...the righteous eateth to the satisfying of his *soul*..." (KJ, NKJ)
"...the righteous *man* eats and is satisfied..." (L)
"...the righteous eat to *their hearts content*..." (NIV)
"...the good *man* eats to live..." (TLB)
"...the righteous has enough to satisfy *his appetite*..." (RV)
(Proverbs 13:25)

"...he that refuseth instruction despiseth *his own soul*..." (KJ)
"...he who disdains instruction despises *his own soul*..." (NKJ)

"...he who refuses instruction despises *his own soul...*" (L)
"...he who ignores discipline despises *himself...*" (NIV)
"...he who ignores instruction despises *himself...*" (RV)
"...to reject criticism is to harm *yourself...*" (TLB)
(Proverbs 15:32)

"...he that keepeth his way preserveth *his soul...*" (KJ)
"...he who keeps is way preserves *his soul...*" (NKJ)
"...he who is careful of *his soul,* safeguards his way..." (L)
"...he who guards his way guards *his life...*" (NIV)
"...he who guards his way preserves *his life...*" (RV)
"...he who follows that path (*he*) is safe..." (TLB)
(Proverbs 16:17)

"...that the *soul* be without knowledge, it is not good..." (KJ)
"...it is not good for a *soul* to be without knowledge..." (NKJ)
"...he who has no knowledge of his own *soul*, it is not good... (L)
"...it is not good (for *anyone*) to have zeal without knowledge..." (NIV)
"...it is dangerous and sinful (for *anyone*) to rush into the unknown..." (TLB)
"...it is not good for a *man* to be without knowledge..." (RV)
(Proverbs 19:2)

"...an idle *soul* shall suffer hunger..." (KJ, RV)
"...an idle *person* will suffer hunger..." (NKJ)
"...a proud *man* shall suffer hunger..." (L)
"...the shiftless *man* goes hungry..." (NIV)
"...a lazy *man*...goes hungry..." (TLB)
(Proverbs 19:15)

"...he that keepeth the commandment keepeth *his own soul...* (KJ)
"...he that keeps the commandments keeps *his soul...*" (NKJ)
"...he who keeps the commandments keeps *his life...*" (RV)
"...he who keeps the law keeps *his soul...*" (L)
"...he who obeys instructions guards *his life...*" (NIV)
"...keep the commandments and keep *our life...*" (TLB)
(Proverbs 19:16)

"...do not let *thy soul* spare for his crying..." (KJ)
"...do not set *your heart* on his destruction..." (NKJ, RV)
"...let not *your soul* share his dishonor..." (L)
"...do not be a willing *party* to his death..." (NIV)
"...*you* will ruin his life..." (TLB)
(Proverbs 19:18)

"...sinneth against *his own soul*..." (KJ)
"...sins against *his own life*..." (NKJ, L)
"...forfeits *his life*..." (NIV, RV)
"...is to risk *your life*..." (TLB)
(Proverbs 20:2)

"...the *soul* of the wicked desireth evil..." (KJ, NKJ, RV)
"...the wicked *man* craves evil..." (NIV)
"...an evil *man* loves to harm others..." (TLB)
(Proverbs 21:10)

"...keepeth *his soul* from troubles..." (KJ)
"...keeps *his soul* from troubles..." (NKJ)
"...keeps *himself* from trouble..." (L, RV)
"...keeps *himself* from calamity..." (NIV)
"...*you'll* stay out of trouble..." (TLB)
(Proverbs 21:23)

"...and spoil the *soul* of them that spoiled them..." (KJ)
"...and plunder the *soul* of those who plunder them..." (NKJ)
"...and will plunder *those* that plunder them..." (NIV)
"...if you injure *them*, he will punish you..." (TLB)
"...and despoil the *life* of those who despoil them..." (RV)
(Proverbs 22:23)

"...and set a snare to *thy soul*..." (KJ, NKJ)
"...and find a stumbling block to *your soul*..." (L)
"...and get *yourself* ensnared..." (NIV)
"...and entangle *yourself* in a snare..." (RV)
"...and endanger *your soul*..." (TLB)
(Proverbs 22:25)

"...and He that keepeth *thy soul*, does He not know it..." (KJ, NKJ)
"...and He who keeps *your soul* knows it..." (L)
"...does not He who guards *your life* know it..." (NIV)
"...and He who watches over *your soul...*" (RV)
"...God...who knows *all hearts...*" (TLB)
(Proverbs 24:12)

"...for he refreshes the *soul* of his master..." (KJ, NKJ, L)
"...for he refreshes the *spirit* of his master..." (NIV, RV)
(Proverbs 25:13)

"...the full *soul* loatheth an honeycomb..." (KJ)
"...a satisfied *soul* loathes the honeycomb..." (NKJ)
"...a *person* who is full loathes a honeycomb" (L)
"...*he* who is full loathes honey..." (NIV)
"...even honey seems tasteless to a *man* who is full..." (TLB)
"...*he* who is sated loathes honey..." (RV)
"...to the hungry *soul*, every bitter thing is sweet..." (KJ)
"...to *him* who is hungry, every bitter thing is sweet..." (LV, RV)
"...if *he* is hungry, *he'll* eat anything..." (LV)
"...to a hungry *soul* every bitter thing is sweet..." (NKJ)
"...to a hungry *person* even a bitter thing is sweet..." (L)
"...to *the hungry*, even what is bitter tastes sweet..." (NIV)
(Proverbs 27:7)

"...but the just seek *his soul...*" (KJ)
"...but the upright seek *his well-being...*" (NKJ)
"...but the righteous have compassion upon *them...*" (L)
"...a wise *man* holds his temper..." (TLB)
"...but the wicked seek *his life...*" (RV)
(Proverbs 29:10)

"...hateth his own *soul...*" (KJ)
"...hates his own *life...* " (NKJ, RV)
"...hates his own *soul...*" (L)
"...is his own *enemy...*" (NIV)
"...must really hate *himself...*" (TLB)
(Proverbs 29:24)

"...and that he should make his *soul* enjoy good in his labour..." (KJ, NKJ, L)
"...than to enjoy *his* food and drink..." (TLB)
"...and find satisfaction in *his* work..." (NIV)
"...than to find enjoyment in *his* toil..." (RV)
(Ecclesiastes 2:24)

"...bereaving *my soul* of good..." (KJ)
"...deprive *myself* of good..." (NKJ)
"...denying *myself* good things..." (L)
"...depriving *myself* of enjoyment..." (NIV)
"...depriving *myself* of pleasure..." (RV)
"...*I*...giving up so much..." (TLB)
(Ecclesiastes 4:8)

"...he wanteth nothing for his *soul*..." (KJ)
"...he lacks nothing for *himself*..." (NKJ)
"...he lacks nothing for *his soul*..." (L)
"...he lacks nothing *his heart* desires..." (NIV)
"...they can have everything *they* want..." (TLB)
"...he lacks nothing of all that *he* desires..." (RV)
(Ecclesiastes 6:2)

"...and *his soul* be not filled..." (KJ, L)
"...*his soul* is not satisfied..." (NKJ)
"...and *he* cannot enjoy..." (NIV)
"...but *he* does not enjoy..." (RV)
"...but (*he*) leaves so little..." (TLB)
(Ecclesiastes 6:3)

"...*my soul* seeketh..." (KJ)
"...*my soul* still seeks..." (NKJ)
"...*my soul* sought..." (L)
"...*I* was still searching..." (NIV)
"...*I* came to this result..." (TLB)
"...*my mind* has sought..." (RV)
(Ecclesiastes 7:28)

"...whom *my soul* loveth..." (KJ)
"...whom *I* love..." (NKJ)
"...whom *my soul* loves..." (L, RV)
"...whom *I* love..." (NIV)
"...O one *I* love..." (TLB)
(Solomon 1:7)

"...I sought him whom *my soul* loveth..." (KJ)
"...I sought the one *I* love..." (NKJ)
"...I sought him who *my soul* loves..." (L)
"...I looked for the one *my heart* loves..." (NIV)
(Solomon 3:1)

"...whom *my soul* loveth..."(KJ)
"...seek the one *I* love..." (NKJ, TLB)
"...*my soul* loves..." (L, RV)
"...the one *my heart* loves..." (NIV)
(Solomon 3:2)

"...saw ye him whom *my soul* loveth?..." (KJ)
"...have you seen the one *I* love?..." (NKJ)
"...have you seen him whom *my soul* loves?..."(L)
"...have you seen the one *my heart* loves?...(NIV)
(Solomon 3:3)

"...whom *my soul* loveth..." (KJ)
"...the one *I* love..." (NKJ, TLB)
"...whom *my soul* loves..." (L, RV)
"...the one *my heart* loves..." (NIV)
(Solomon 3:4)

"...*my soul* failed when he spake..." (KJ, RV)
"...*my heart* leaped up when he spoke..." (NKJ)
"...*my heart* failed when he spoke..." (L)
"...*my heart* sank at his departure..." (NIV)
"...*my heart* stopped..." (TLB)
(Solomon 5:6)

"...*my soul* made me like the chariots of Amminadib..." (KJ)
"...*my soul* had made me as the chariots of my noble people..." (NKJ)
"...*I* sat in the public chariot which was ready..." (L)
"...*my desires* set me among the royal chariots of my people..." (NIV)
"...*my fancy* set me in a chariot beside my prince..." (RV)
"...*I* was stricken with terrible homesickness..." (TLB)
(Solomon 6:12)

"...woe unto *their soul*..." (KJ, NKJ, L)
"...woe to *them*..." (NIV, RV)
"...what a catastrophe! *They* have doomed themselves..." (TLB)
(Isaiah 3:9)

"...the desire of our *soul*..." (KJ, NKJ, L, RV)
"...the desire of our *hearts*..." (NIV)
"...our *hearts* desire..." (TLB)
(Isaiah 26:8)

"...and *his soul* is empty..." (KJ)
"...and his *soul* is still empty..." (NKJ)
"...and *he* is weary and famished..." (L)
"...and *his hunger* remains..." (NIV)
"...with *his hunger* unsatisfied..." (RV)
"...but (*a man*) is still hungry..." (TLB)
"...and *his soul* has appetite..." (KJ)
"...and *his soul* still craves..." (NKJ)
"...and *his thirst* not quenched..." (L, RV)
"...with *his thirst* unquenched..." (NIV)
"...*he* is faint and craving..." (TLB)
(Isaiah 29:8)

"...to *make empty the soul of the hungry*..." (KJ, L)
"...to *keep the hungry unsatisfied*..." (NKJ)
"...*the hungry* he leaves empty ..." (NIV)
"...an *evil man*...their *cheating of the hungry*..." (TLB)
(Isaiah 32:6)

"...in love for *my soul* delivered it..." (KJ)

"...lovingly delivered *my soul*..." (NKJ)
"...lovingly delivered *me*..." (TLB)
"...in your love you kept *me*..." (NIV)
"...thou has cast *my sins* behind my back..." (RV)
(Isaiah 38:17)

"...in whom *My soul* delighteth..." (KJ)
"...in whom *My soul* delights..." (NKJ, L, RV)
"...My chosen One in whom *I* delight..." (NIV)
"...in whom *I* delight..." (TLB)
(Isaiah 42:1)

"...he cannot deliver *his soul*..." (KJ, NKJ)
"...and cannot deliver *themselves*..." (L)
"...he cannot save *himself*..." (NIV)
"...he cannot bring *himself* to ask..." (TLB)
"...he cannot deliver *himself*..." (RV)
(Isaiah 44:20)

"...which have said to *thy soul*..." (KJ)
"...which have said to *you*..." (NKJ)
"...who have said to *your soul*..." (L)
"...who said to *you*..." (NIV)
"...those who tormented *you*..." (TLB)
"...of *your* tormentors..." (RV)
(Isaiah 51:23)

"...make *his soul* an offering to sin..." (KJ)
"...make *His soul* an offering for sin..." (NKJ, TLB)
"...*His life* as an offering for sin..." (L)
"...*His life* a guilt offering..." (NIV)
"...makes *Himself* and offering for sin..." (RV)
(Isaiah 53:10)

"...He hath poured out *His soul* unto death..." (KJ, NKJ, TLB)
"...He has poured out *His life* to death..." (L, RV)
"...He poured out *His life* into death..." (NIV)
(Isaiah 53:12)

"...we afflicted *our soul*..." (KJ)
"...we afflicted *our souls*..." (NKJ)
"...we afflicted *ourselves*..." (L)
"...we humbled *ourselves*..." (NIV, RV)
"...why aren't you impressed (with what *we've* done)..." (TLB)
(Isaiah 58:3)

"...a day for a man to afflict *his soul*..." (KJ, NKJ, L)
"...a day for a man to humble *himself*..." (NIV, RV)
"...a man to bow down *his head*..." (TLB)
(Isaiah 58:5)

"...if thou draw out thy *soul* to the hungry..." (KJ)
"...if you extend your *soul* to the hungry..." (NKJ)
"...if you give *your* bread to the hungry..." (L)
"...pour *yourselves* out to the hungry..." (RV)
"...and satisfy the afflicted *soul*..." (KJ, NKJ, L)
"...spend *yourselves* in behalf of the hungry..." (NIV)
"...and if *(you)* satisfy the desires of the afflicted..." (RV)
"...(You) feed the hungry. Help those in trouble..." (TLB)
(Isaiah 58:10)

"...satisfy thy *soul* in drought..." (KJ)
"...satisfy your *soul* in drought..." (NKJ)
"...satisfy your *soul* with rich food..." (L)
"...satisfy *your* need in a sun-scorched land..." (NIV)
"...satisfy *you* with all good things..." (TLB)
"...satisfy *your* desire with good things..." (RV)
(Isaiah 58:11)

"...whereas the sword reaches into the *soul*..." (KJ)
"...whereas the sword reaches into the *heart*..." (NKJ)
"...the sword reaches into the *soul*..." (L)
"...when the sword is at our *throats*..." (NIV)
"...the sword is even now poised to strike *them* dead..." (TLB)
"...whereas the sword has reached *their very life*..." (RV)
(Jeremiah 4:10)

"...because thou hast heard, O *my soul*..." (KJ)
"...because you have heard, Oh *my soul*..." (NKJ)
"...because *my soul* has heard..." (L)
"...for *I* have heard..." (NIV, TLB)
"...for *I* hear..." (RV)
(Jeremiah 4:19)

"...*my soul* is wearied..." (KJ)
"...*my soul* is weary..." (NKJ)
"...*my soul* faints..." (L)
"...*my life* is given over..." (NIV)
"...*my people* are gasping..." (TLB)
"...*I* am fainting..." (RV)
(Jeremiah 4:31)

"...shall not *my soul* be avenged..." (KJ, TLB)
"...shall I not avenge *myself*..." (NKJ, L, RV)
"...should I not avenge *myself*..." (NIV, RV)
"...shall I not send *my* vengeance..." (TLB)
(Jeremiah 5:9, 29; 9:9)

"...lest *My soul* depart from thee..." (KJ)
"...lest *My soul* depart from you..." (NKJ)
"...lest *My soul* abhor you..." (L)
"...or *I* will turn away from you..." (NIV)
"...lest *I* be alienated from you..." (RV)
"...*I* will empty the land..." (TLB)
(Jeremiah 6:8)

"...the dearly beloved of *my soul*..." (KJ, NKJ, L, RV)
"...the one *I* love..." (NIV)
"...*my* dearest ones..." (TLB)
(Jeremiah 12:7)

"...*my soul* shall weep..." (KJ, NKJ, L)
"...*I* will weep..." (NIV)

"...*my breaking heart* will mourn..." (TLB)
"...*my eyes* will weep bitterly..." (RV)
(Jeremiah 13:17)

"...hath *thou soul* loathed Zion..." (KJ, L)
"...has *your soul* loathed Zion..." (NKJ, RV)
"...do *you* despise Zion..." (NIV)
"...do *you* abhor Jerusalem..." (TLB)
(Jeremiah 14:19)

"...for they have digged a pit for *my soul*..." (KJ, L)
"...for they have dug a pit for *my life*..." (NKJ, RV)
"...they have dug a pit for *me*..." (NIV)
"...they have set a trap to kill *me*..." (TLB)
(Jeremiah 18:20)

"...for He hath delivered the *soul* ..." (KJ)
"...for He has delivered the *life*..." (NKJ, L, RV)
"...He rescues the *life*..." (NIV, TLB)
(Jeremiah 20:13)

"...and *their soul* shall be as a watered garden..." (KJ, L)
"...and *their life* shall be like a watered garden..." (TLB, RV)
"...*their soul* shall be like a well watered garden..." (NKJ)
"...*they* will be like a well watered garden..." (NIV)
(Jeremiah 31:12)

"...the *soul of the priests* with fatness..." (KJ, L)
"...the *soul of the priests* with abundance..." (NKJ)
"...satisfy *the priests* with abundance..." (NIV, RV)
"...I will feast *the priests* with abundance..." (TLB)
(Jeremiah 31:14)

"...I have satiated the *weary soul*..." (KJ, NKJ)
"...I have satisfied the *thirsty soul*..." (L)
"...I will refresh *the weary*..." (NIV)
"...I have given rest to *the weary*..." (TLB)

"...I will satisfy the *weary soul...*" (RV)
(Jeremiah 31:25)

"...I have replenished every *sorrowful soul...*" (KJ, NKJ)
"...I have replenished every *hungry soul...*" (L)
"...I will...satisfy *the faint...*" (NIV)
"...*every soul* I will replenish..." (RV)
"...I have given...joy to *all the suffering...*" (TLB)
(Jeremiah 31:25)

"...that made us this *soul...*" (KJ)
"...who made our very *souls...*" (NKJ, RV)
"...who created *soul* in us..." (L)
"...who has given us *breath...*" (NIV)
"...Almighty God *his* creator..." (TLB)
(Jeremiah 38:16)

"...*thy soul* shall live..." (KJ)
"...*your soul* shall live..." (NKJ)
"...*you* will spare your life..." (L)
"...*your life* will be spared..." (NIV, RV)
"...you and your family *shall live...*" (TLB)
(Jeremiah 38:17)

"...and *thy soul* shall live..." (KJ, NKJ)
"...and *your life* shall be saved..." (L)
"...and *your life* will be spared..." (NIV, TLB, RV)
(Jeremiah 38:20)

"...and *his soul* shall be satisfied..." (KJ, NKJ, L)
"...and *his (Israel's) appetite* shall be satisfied..." (NIV)
"...and (*Israel*) to be happy once more..." (TLB)
"...and *his* (Israel's) *desire* shall be satisfied..." (RV)
(Jeremiah 50:19)

"...deliver every man *his soul...*" (KJ)
"...everyone save *his life...*" (NKJ)
"...let every man save *his life...*" (L)

"...run for *your lives*..." (NIV)
(Jeremiah 51:6)

"...deliver every man *his soul*..." (KJ)
"...let everyone deliver *himself*..." (NKJ)
"...spare every man *his life*..." (L)
"...run for *your lives*..." (NIV)
(Jeremiah 51:45)

"...they have given their pleasant things for meat to relieve the *soul*..." (KJ)
"...they have given their valuables for food to restore *life*..." (NKJ)
"...they have given their precious things for food to relieve the *soul*..." (L)
"...they barter their treasures for food to keep *themselves* alive..." (NIV)
(Lamentations 1:11)

"...the Comforter that should relieve *my soul*..." (KJ, L)
"...the Comforter who should restore *my life*..." (NKJ)
"...no one is near to comfort *me*..." (NIV)
(Lamentations 1:16)

"...when *their soul* was poured out..." (KJ, L)
"...when *their life* is poured out..." (NKJ)
"...as *their lives* ebb away..." (NIV, TLB)
"...and *their life* is poured out..." (RV)
(Lamentations 2:12)

"...removed *my soul* far off from peace..." (KJ, NKJ)
"...*my soul* has gone astray from peace..." (L)
"...*I* have been deprived of peace..." (NIV)
"...you have taken them away (from *me*)..." (TLB)
"...*my soul* is bereft of peace ..." (RV)
(Lamentations 3:17)

"...*my soul* hath them still in remembrance..." (KJ)
"...*my soul* still remembers..." (NKJ)
"...remember and restore *my life*..." (L)
"...*I* will remember them..." (NIV)
"...*I* can never forget..." (TLB)
"...*my soul* continually thinks of it..." (RV)
(Lamentations 3:20)

"...saith *my soul*..." (KJ)
"...says *my soul*..." (NKJ, L)
"...I say to *myself*..." (NIV)
"...*my soul* claims the Lord..." (TLB)
"...the Lord is *my* portion..." (RV)
(Lamentations 3:24)

"...to *the soul* that seeketh Him..." (KJ)
"...to *the soul* who seeks Him..." (NKJ, L)
"...to *the one* who seeks Him..." (NIV)
"...to *those* who wait for Him..." (TLB, RV)
(Lamentations 3:25)

"...Thou hast pleaded the causes of *my soul*..." (KJ)
"...You have pleaded the case for *my soul*..." (NKJ)
"...Thou hast pleaded *my cause*..." (L)
"...You took up *my case*..." (NIV)
"...plead *my* case..." (TLB)
"...Thou hast redeemed *my life*..." (RV)
(Lamentations 3:58)

"...thou hast delivered *thou soul*..." (KJ)
"...you have delivered *your soul*..." (NKJ, L)
"...you will have saved *yourself*..." (NIV)
"...but *you* are blameless..." (TLB)
"...but you will have saved *your life*..." (RV)
(Ezekiel 3:19)

"...thou hast delivered *thy soul*..." (KJ)
"...you will have delivered *your soul*..." (NKJ, L)

"...you will have saved *yourself...*" (NIV)
"...you will have saved *your own life...*" (TLB)
"...you will have saved *your life...*" (RV)
(Ezekiel 3:21)

"...*my soul* hath not been polluted..." (KJ)
"...I have never defiled *myself...*" (NKJ, L, NIV, RV)
"...*I* have never been defiled..." (TLB)
(Ezekiel 4:14)

"...he shall save *his soul* alive..." (KJ)
"...he preserves *himself* alive..." (NKJ)
"...saves *his soul* alive..." (L)
"...he will save *his life...*" (NIV, RV)
"...he shall save *his soul...*" (TLB)
(Ezekiel 18:27)

"...and *her mind* was alienated from them..." (KJ)
"...and alienated *herself* from them..." (NKJ)
"...then *her soul* abhorred them..." (L)
"...*she* turned away from them in disgust..." (NIV, RV)
"...*she* hated them..." (TLB)
(Ezekiel 23:17)

"...that which *your soul* pitieth..." (KJ)
"...the delight of *your soul...*" (NKJ)
"...the desire of *your soul...*" (RV)
"...the cleanser of *your soul...*" (L)
"...the delight of *your eyes...*" (NIV)
"...the strength of *your nation...*" (TLB)
"...the desire of *your soul...*" (RV)
(Ezekiel 24:21)

"...shall deliver *his soul...*" (KJ)
"...will save *his life...*" (NKJ)
"...he shall deliver *his life...*" (L)
"...would have saved *himself...*" (NIV)

"...would have saved *his life...*" (TLB, RV)
(Ezekiel 33:5)

"...but thou hast delivered *thy soul...*" (KJ)
"...but you have delivered *your soul...*" (NKJ, L)
"...but you have saved *yourself...*" (NIV)
"...and *you* will not be responsible..." (TLB)
"...but you will have saved *your life...*" (RV)
(Ezekiel 33:9)

"...their bread for *their soul...*" (KJ)
"...their bread shall be for *their own life...*" (NKJ)
"...for *their own* bread..." (L)
"...this food shall be for *themselves...*" (NIV, TLB)
"...their bread will be only for *their hunger...*" (RV)
(Hosea 9:4)

"...the waters compassed me, even to *the soul...*" (KJ)
"...the waters surrounded me, even to *my soul...*" (NKJ)
"...the waters engulfed me, even to *the soul...*" (L)
"...the deep surrounded me, the seaweed wrapped around *my head...*" (NIV)
"...the waters closed above *me...*" (TLB)
"...the waters closed in over *me...*" (RV)
(Jonah 2:5)

"...when *my soul* fainted within me..." (KJ, NKJ, L, RV)
"...when *my life* was ebbing away..." (NIV)
"...when *I* had lost all hope..." (TLB)
(Jonah 2:7)

"...*my soul* desired..." (KJ)
"...*my soul* desires..." (NKJ, RV)
"...*my soul* craves..." (L)
"...that *I* crave..." (NIV)
"...*I* long for it..." (TLB)
(Micah 7:1)

"…*his soul*…is not upright…" (KJ, NKJ, RV)
"…*his soul* does not delight in iniquity…" (L)
"…*his desires* are not upright…" (NIV)
"…*wicked men* fail…" (TLB)
(Habakkuk 2:4)

"…and hast sinned against *thy soul*…" (KJ)
"…and sin against *your soul*…" (NKJ)
"…caused *your soul* to sin…" (L)
"…and forfeiting *your life*…" (NIV)
"…you have forfeited *your own life*…" (TLB, RV)
(Habakkuk 2:10)

"…the shephards…*my soul* loathed them…" (KJ, NKJ)
"…*my soul* was wearied of them…" (L)
"…and *I* grew weary of them…" (NIV)
"…*I* became impatient with them…" (RV)
"…*I* became impatient with these sheep…" (TLB)
(Zechariah 11:8)

"…and *their soul* also abhorred me…" (KJ, NKJ)
"…and *they* hated me too…" (TLB)
"…and *their souls* also howled against me…" (L)
"…*the flock* detested me…" (NIV)
"…and *they* also detested me…" (RV)
(Zechariah 11:8)

TRANSLATIONS FROM THE NEW TESTAMENT FOLLOW:

"…fear not them which kill the body, but are not able to kill the *soul;* but rather fear Him which is able to destroy both body and *soul in hell*…" (KJ, NKJ, RV)
"…do not be afraid of those who kill the body but cannot kill the *soul*. Rather, be afraid of the One who can destroy both *soul* and body in hell…" (NIV)
"…do not be afraid o those who kill the body but cannot kill the

soul. But above all, be afraid of the One who can destroy both the *soul* and the body in hell…" (L)

"…be not afraid of those who can kill only your bodies – but can't touch your *souls*! Fear only God who can destroy both *soul* and body in hell…" (TLB)

"…be not afraid of those who kill the body, but cannot destroy the *life*; but rather fear Him who can utterly destroy both *life* and body in Gehenna…" (D)

(Matthew 10:28)

"…you will find rest for *your souls*…" (KJ, NKJ, NIV, L, TLB, RV)

"…and *your lives* will find a resting place…" (D)

(Matthew 11:29)

"…in whom *My soul* is well pleased…" (KJ, NKJ, RV)

"…in whom *I* delight…" (NIV)

"…in whom *My soul* delights…" (TLB)

"…in whom *My soul* rejoices…" (L)

"…in whom *I* take delight…" (D)

(Matthew 12:18)

"…what is a man profited, if he shall gain the whole world, and lose *his own soul…*" (KJ, NKJ)

"…what good will it be for a man if he gains the whole world, yet forfeits *his soul…*" (NIV)

"…for how would a man be benefitted, if he should gain the whole world and lose *his own soul…*" (L)

"…for what advantage would a man have if he acquires the whole world and forfeits *his own life…*" (RV, D)

"…what profit is there if you gain the whole world – and lose *eternal life…*" (TLB)

(Matthew 16:26; Mark 8:36)

"…what will a man give in exchange for *his soul…*" (KJ, NKJ, NIV, L)

"…what can compare to the value of *eternal life…*" (TLB)

"…what shall a man give in exchange for *his life…*" (RV)

"…what will a man give in ransom for *his life…*" (D)

(Matthew 16:26; Mark 8:37)

"...with all the *soul*..." (KJ, NKJ, L)
"...with all your *heart*..." (NIV, TLB, RV)
"...with all the *understanding*..." (D)
(Mark 12:33)

"...*My soul* magnifies the Lord..." (KJ, NKJ, L)
"...*My soul* glorifies the Lord..." (NIV)
"...Oh how *I* praise the Lord..." (TLB)
"...*My soul* extols the Lord..." (D)
(Luke 1:46)

"...and I will say to *my soul*..." (KJ, NKJ, RV)
"...and I shall say to *myself*..." (L, NIV, D)
"...and I will sit back and say to *myself*..." (TLB)
(Luke 12:19)

"...*Soul*, thou hast much goods..." (KJ)
"...*Soul*, you have many goods..." (NKJ)
"...*You* have many good things..." (L)
"...*You* have plenty of good things..." (NIV)
"...*Friend*, you have enough..." (TLB)
"...*Soul*, you have ample goods..." (RV)
"...*Life*, thou hast an abundance..." (D)
(Luke 12:19)

"...*thy soul* shall be required of thee..." (KJ, NKJ, RV)
"...*your life* will be demanded of you..." (L, NIV, D)
"...tonight *you* will die..." (TLB)
(Luke 12:20)

"...in your patience possess ye *your souls*..." (KJ, NKJ)
"...by your patience you will gain *your souls*..." (L)
"...standing firm you will gain *life*..." (NIV)
"...if you stand firm, you will win *your souls*..." (TLB)
"...by your endurance you will gain *your lives*..." (RV)
"...by your patient endurance preserve *your lives*..." (D)
(Luke 21:19)

"...now is *my soul* troubled..." (KJ, TLB, RV, D)
"...now *my soul* is troubled..." (NKJ)
"...now *my soul* is disturbed..." (L)
"...now *my heart* is troubled..." (NIV)
(John 12:27)

"...thou wilt not leave *my soul* in hell..." (KJ)
"...you will not leave *my soul* in hades..." (NKJ)
"...you will not leave *my soul* in shoel..." (L)
"...because thou wilt not abandon *my soul...*" (RV, D)
"...you will not leave *my soul* in hell..." (TLB)
"...because you will not abandon *me* to the grave..." (NIV)
(Acts 2:27)

"...*His soul* (Christ's) was not left in hell..." (KJ)
"...*His soul* (Christ's) was not left in hades..." (NKJ, RV, D)
"...*His soul* (Christ's) was not left in the grave..." (L)
"...*He* (Christ) was not abandoned to the grave..." (NIV)
(Acts 2:31)

"...there were added to them about 3000 *souls...*" (KJ, NKJ)
"...and about 3000 *souls* were added..." (L, RV, D)
"...3000 (*converts)...*baptized were added to their number..." (NIV)
"...*those* baptized...were about 3000 in all..." (TLB)
(Acts 2:41)

"...fear came upon *every soul...*" (KJ, NKJ, L, RV, D)
"...*everyone* was filled with awe..." (NIV)
"...a deep sense of awe was on *them all...*" (TLB)
(Acts 2:43)

"...*every soul* which will not hear..." (KJ, NKJ)
"...*every person* who will not listen..." (L)
"...*anyone* who does not listen..." (NIV)
"...*every soul* that will not listen..." (RV)
"...*anyone* who will not listen..." (TLB)
"...*every soul* which may not hear..." (D)
(Acts 3:23)

"...were of one heart and *one soul*..." (KJ, NKJ)
"...were of *one soul* and *one mind*..." (L)
"...were of *one heart* and *one mind*..." (NIV, TLB)
"...were one in heart and *soul*..." (RV)
"...the heart and *soul* was one..." (D)
(Acts 4:32)

"...threescore and fifteen *souls*..." (KJ)
"...seventy five *people*..." (NKJ)
"...seventy five *souls*..." (L, RV, D)
"...whole *family*, seventy five in all..." (NIV)
"...seventy five *persons*..." (TLB)
(Acts 7:14)

"...Confirming the *souls* of the disciples..." (KJ, D)
"...strengthening the *souls* of the disciples..." (NKJ, RV)
"...strengthening the *souls* of the converts..." (L)
"...strengthening the *disciples* and encouraging them..." (NIV)
"...they helped the *believers* to grow..." (TLB)
(Acts 14:22)

"...subverting your *souls*..." (KJ)
"...unsettling your *souls*..." (NKJ, L)
"...unsettling your *minds*..." (RV, D)
"...troubling your *minds*..." (NIV)
"...questioned your *salvation*..." (TLB)
(Acts 15:24)

"...two hundred threescore and sixteen *souls*..." (KJ)
"...two hundred seventy six *persons*..." (NKJ)
"...there were 276 of *us*..." (NIV, TLB)
"...two hundred and seventy six *persons*..." (L, RV)
"...all the *souls* were two hundred and seventy six..." (D)
(Acts 27:37)

"...upon *every soul* of man..." (KJ)
"...on every *soul of man*..." (NKJ, D)
"...for *every man*..." (L)

"...for every *human...*" (NIV)
"...for *Jews and Gentiles* alike..." (TLB)
"...for *every human being...*" (RV)
(Romans 2:9)

"...*every soul* be subject unto higher powers..." (KJ)
"...*every soul* be subject to the governing authorities..." (NKJ)
"...*every soul* be subject to the sovereign authorities..." (L)
"...*everyone* must submit to the governing authorities..." (NIV)
"...*(everyone)* obey the government..." (TLB)
"...*every person* be subject to the governing authority..." (RV)
"...*every person* be subject to the superior authority..." (D)
(Romans 13:1)

"...Adam was made a *living soul...*" (KJ, L)
"...the first man became a *living being...*" (NKJ)
"...Adam became a *living being...*" (NIV, RV, D)
"...Adam was given a *living, human body...*" (TLB)
(1 Corinthians 15:45)

"...for a record upon *my soul...*" (KJ)
"...as a witness against *my soul...*" (NKJ)
"...to God concerning *myself...*" (L)
"...God as *my* witness..." (NIV)
"...God to witness against *me...*" (TLB, RV)
"...as a witness to *my soul...*" (D)
(2 Corinthians 1:23)

"...but also *our souls...*" (KJ)
"...but also *our own lives...*" (NKJ, TLB)
"...but even *our lives...*" (L)
"...but *our lives* as well..." (NIV)
"...but also *our own selves...*" (RV, D)
(1 Thessalonians 2:8)

"...dividing asunder of *soul and spirit...*" (KJ)
"...piercing even to the division of *spirit and soul...*" (NKJ, L, RV)
"...even to dividing *soul and spirit...*" (NIV)

"...cutting into our innermost *thoughts and desires*..." (TLB)
"...cutting through even to a separation of *Life and Breath*..." (D)
(Hebrews 4:12)

"...as an anchor of *the soul*..." (KJ, NKJ, NIV, TLB, RV)
"...like an anchor to *us*..." (L)
"...an anchor of the *life*..." (D)
(Hebrews 6:19)

"...*My soul* shall have no pleasure in him..." (KJ, NKJ, L, RV)
"...*I* will not be pleased with him..." (NIV)
"...*God* will have no pleasure in them..." (TLB)
"...*My soul* does not delight in him..." (D)
(Hebrews 10:38)

"...believe to the saving of *the soul*..." (KJ, NKJ)
"...faith which restores *our souls*..." (L)
"...those who *believe and are saved*..." (NIV)
"...faith in Him assures *our souls'* salvation..." (TLB)
"...faith to keep *their souls*..." (RV)
"...faith in order to a preservation of *life*..." (D)
(Hebrews 10:39)

"...they watch for *your souls*..." (KJ)
"...they watch out for *your souls*..." (NKJ)
"...they are watchful guardians for *your souls*..." (L)
"...watch over *your souls*..." (TLB, RV)
"...keep watch on *your behalf*..." (D)
(Hebrews 13:17)

"...which is able to save *your souls*..."(KJ, NKJ, L, TLB, RV, D)
"...which can save *you*..." (NIV)
(James 1:21)

"...shall save *a soul* from death..." (KJ, NKJ, L, RV, D)
"...will save *him* from death..." (NIV)
"...will have saved a wandering *soul* from death..." (TLB)
(James 5:20)

"....salvation of *your soul...*" (KJ, NKJ, L, NIV, TLB, RV)
"...your *salvation...*" (D)
(1 Peter 1:9)

"...ye have purified *your souls...*" (KJ, NKJ)
"...let *your souls* be sanctified..." (L)
"...you have purified *yourselves...*" (NIV)
"...*your souls* have been cleansed..." (TLB)
"...having purified *your souls...*" (RV)
"...having purified *your lives...*" (D)
(1 Peter 1:22)

"...for they fight against *your very souls...*" (TLB)
"...which war against *the soul...*" (KJ, NKJ, L, NIV, RV)
"...which wage war against *the life...*" (D)
(1 Peter 2:11)

"...Shepherd and Bishop of *your souls...*" (KJ)
"...Shepherd and Overseer of *your souls...*" (NKJ, NIV)
"...Shepherd and Guardian of *your souls...*" (L, TLB, RV)
"...Shepherd and Guardian of *your lives...*" (D)
(1 Peter 2:25)

"...eight *souls* were saved by water..." (KJ)
"...eight *souls* were saved through water..." (NKJ)
"...eight *souls* entered into it..." (L)
"...a few *people*, eight in all, were saved..." (NIV)
"...eight *persons* were saved..." (TLB, RV)
"...eight *persons* were carried safely..." (D)
(1 Peter 3:20)

"...the keeping of *their souls* to *him...*" (KJ)
"...commit *their souls* to Him..." (NKJ, L)
"...commit *themselves* to their faithful Creator..." (NIV)
"...trust *yourself* to the God who make you..." (TLB)
"...entrust *your souls* to the faithful Creator..." (RV)
"...commit *your lives* in doing good to a Faithful Creator..." (D)
(1 Peter 4:19)

"...vexed in his *righteous soul*..." (KJ, D)
"...tormented his *righteous soul*..." (NKJ)
"...his *righteous soul* was vexed..." (L)
"...was tormented in his *righteous soul*...(NIV, RV)
"...*a good man*, sick of the terrible wickedness he saw..." (TLB)
(2 Peter 2:8)

"...beguiling *unstable souls*..." (KJ, L)
"...enticing *unstable souls*..." (NKJ)
"...seduce *the unstable*..." (NIV)
"...luring *unstable women*..." (TLB)
"...entice *unsteady souls*..." (RV)
"...alluring *unstable souls*..." (D)
(2 Peter 2:14)

"...the *souls* of them that were slain..." (KJ, L)
"...the *souls* of those who had been slain..." (NKJ, NIV, RV)
"...the *souls* of those who had been martyred..." (TLB)
"...the *persons* of those who had been killed..." (D)
(Revelation 6:9)

"...every *living soul* died in the sea..." (KJ, L, D)
"...very *living creature* in the sea died..." (NKJ)
"...every *living thing* in the sea died..." (NIV, RV)
"...*everything* in all the oceans died..." (TLB)
(Revelation 16:3)

"...and *souls* of men..." (KJ, NKJ, NIV, TLB)
"...and hides and *slaves*..." (L)
"...human *souls*..." (RV)
"...and *lives* of men..." (D)
(Revelation 18:13)

"...the fruit that *thy soul* lusted after..." (KJ, L)
"...the fruit that *your soul* longed for..." (NKJ)
"...the fruit *you* longed for..." (NIV)
"...the fruit for which *your soul* longed..." (RV)

"...the fancy things that *you* loved so much..." (TLB)
"...the fruit season of *thy soul's* ardent desire..." (D)
(Revelation 18:14)

"...the *souls* of them that were beheaded..." (KJ, NKJ, L, NIV, TLB, RV)
"...the *persons* of those who had been beheaded..." (D)
(Revelation 20:4)

Having examined all of the times that the word(s) "soul" "souls" or "soul's" appears in the Bible, I find only that it means a mortal or mortals...a living being or beings...breathing creatures. I invite anyone who believes in *an immortal soul that flies off to heaven when they die* to find a scripture to support such a belief.

Printed in the United States
30309LVS00005B/76-102